SECTIONED: SOCIAL SERVICES AND THE 1983 MENTAL HEALTH ACT

Marian Barnes,
Ric Bowl,

and

Mike Fisher

ROUTLEDGE

First published 1990
by Routledge
11 New Fetter Lane, London EC4P 4EE

© 1990 Marian Barnes, Ric Bowl, and Mike Fisher

Typeset by Laserscript Limited, Mitcham, Surrey
Printed and bound in Great Britain by
Biddles Ltd, Guildford and King's Lynn

British Library Cataloguing in Publication Data

Barnes, Marian, *1952 –*
Sectioned : Social services and the 1983 Mental Health Act.
1. England. Mentally ill persons. Treatment. Law : Mental Health Act
1983
I. Title II. Bowl, Ric, III. Fisher, Mike,
344.204'44

ISBN 0-415-01079-9

CONTENTS

ACKNOWLEDGEMENTS

This book is the result of the collaborative efforts and support of a very large number of people, the majority of whom we do not know by name. Workers in 42 social services departments provided the data on which results and conclusions are based. Liaison officers in those departments ensured that communication flowed between those workers and the central steering group. Members of the SSRG Steering Group: Julie Jones, Mike Lindsey, Mike Lodge, Josephine O'Gorman, David Phillips, Colin Robertshaw, Andrew Rust, Stuart Turnock, Colin Whittington, and at a later stage, Phillip Bowell and Ken Coleman, were all part of the team who conceived, designed, and carried out the research project. All contributed in vital ways to the overall success of this initiative by the Social Services Research Group.

The project was financed by contributions from the participating departments and by grants from the Department of Health and Social Security and the Joseph Rowntree Memorial Trust. We are grateful not only for their financial support, but also for their willingness to back an innovative approach to the conduct of research. The money from DHSS enabled us to employ Di Davies and then Sue Pomlett to assist in the huge administrative tasks and data analysis. Both have seen green forms in their sleep – thanks to them for retaining their humour amongst it all, and thanks also to Birmingham University for providing a base.

Finally we have to note that we have had even less contact with those on the receiving end of social work assessments than we have with the workers themselves. Our hope is that this study will be the source of indirect benefit to those most closely affected by the legislative requirements of the Mental Health Act, 1983.

Chapter 1

COLLABORATION IN THE STUDY OF NEW LEGISLATION

The research project from which this book derives has been an unusual one both in its subject matter and in the way in which it was undertaken. Its origins were in the concerns of social services managers that the Mental Health Act, 1983 was yet another piece of legislation placing new demands on already overstretched resources. The early 1980s had seen a number of significant new pieces of welfare legislation that demanded time to be devoted to understanding their requirements, training for staff involved in implementation, and the establishment of new procedures, if not new resources: the 1980 Child Care Act, the 1980 Foster Children Act, the 1980 Residential Homes Act, the 1982 Juvenile Justice Act, the 1983 Health and Social Services and Social Security Adjudications Act, the 1984 Registered Homes Act, and the 1984 Data Protection Act.

The Mental Health Act, 1983 required attention to be focused on an aspect of the personal social services that rarely achieved any priority. It appeared to imply an expansion of mental health resources to make it possible to prevent hospital admission and to provide aftercare following discharge, it generated an immediate need for substantial new training programmes and procedures to approve formally a new type of designated social worker, and it appeared to open up the activities of social services workers undertaking duties under the legislation to much greater public scrutiny than before. We discuss in some detail the expectations that accompanied the passage of the Act in Chapter 3.

Concern about both the direct resource implications of the Act and about the potential indirect effect it would have on other services by diverting attention away from what were normally

1

regarded as priority areas led to decisions to set up internal systems within some social services departments to monitor the impact of the new Act. Thus one important characteristic of the genesis of this project was a somewhat defensive, but understandable, concern about the time and resource costs of its implementation. More generally a concern was developing both within the social services research community, and amongst those responsible for putting into practice new policy decisions, that new policy directions were being determined centrally, often embodied in legislation, with no attempt being made to monitor what effect this was having either on those responsible for implementing decisions or on recipients of services who should be the ultimate beneficiaries of policy development.

In 1983 representatives of the Social Services Research Group (SSRG) and of the Association of Directors of Social Services (ADSS) met to discuss research priorities and it was agreed that the impact of new legislation was one area that should be given priority. As well as identifying priority topic areas, these discussions also highlighted the repetitive and unco-ordinated nature of much of the research undertaken within social services departments and suggested that priority areas would benefit from a common approach. Thus when it became obvious that a number of departments were starting to set up individual systems to monitor the implementation of the Mental Health Act, 1983, a group of SSRG members got together to propose a common system in which all interested departments could be involved.

Thus the first unusual feature of the project was that it was designed and undertaken by a group of researchers, the majority of whom were employed as full-time researchers within social services departments. As such it represents an example of the benefits of large-scale collaboration across social services departments and between those departments and the university departments that were also represented in the group (see Barnes,1987). It did not depend on a large research grant that had to be negotiated before the project could start. Rather, it was launched by all those departments that wanted to become involved ' buying in' by contributing a small fee to meet non-personnel costs of the project and committing staff time to varying degrees for the purposes of administration, data collection, and analysis.

2

This model of research has considerable advantages in terms of achieving immediate and specific relevance for those operational agencies that became involved, *and* providing a comparative overview of the picture across the country. However, from another perspective, the fact that monitoring the implementation of new legislation was left to local initiative and was dependent on individual researchers and individual directors of social services being willing to accord priority and time to the project, can be seen as an example of the State's somewhat ambivalent attitude towards social policy. New social welfare legislation is passed with few consistent attempts to determine what impact it has on the lives of those it is designed to affect, in spite of Seebohm's caution that the new personal social services departments would be 'experiments' in meeting social need and as such should be evaluated to ensure that the experiments were achieving what was intended (Seebohm, 1968). Once the project was underway, additional financial support was provided by both the Department of Health and Social Security (DHSS) and the Joseph Rowntree Memorial Trust and this enabled the project to be further developed. Considerable interest in the findings has been expressed by the DHSS, but it is far from certain that such a project would have been initiated from within the government department responsible for the oversight of social welfare legislation.

All social services departments in England and Wales were invited to join the project (the main provisions of the 1983 Act did not extend to Scotland or to Northern Ireland). The response was larger than expected: of a total of 117 social services departments in England and Wales, 42 departments joined the project and collected the data that forms the basis of the following discussion. These 42 departments (36 per cent of the total) were from all parts of the country and included 13 English shire counties, 15 metropolitan districts, and 13 London boroughs. Some 16 million (34%) of the 47 million people in England and Wales in 1985 were covered. The distribution according to type of SSD is shown as follows (excluding the Isle of Wight and Channel Island Authorities). Whilst they were self-selected, the size and distribution of the sample authorities is sufficient to have confidence that the picture they present is not likely to be an unusual one. The size of the response necessitated establishing a structure to deal with administration and liaison. Members of the central steering group took on responsibility for liaising with groups of departments on a regional basis and each individual department was asked to nominate a local liaison officer to act as contact point.

Table 1.1

	SSRG	All	%
London boroughs	13	33	39.4
Metropolitan district councils	15	36	41.7
English county councils	13	38	34.2
Wales	1	8	12.5

Thus, distribution of data-collection forms, instructions, notification of meetings and feedback devolved from the centre to regional liaison officers and thence to individual departments. The regional liaison officer was the first point of contact if there were queries about the project in general or any specific queries about particular aspects of data collection. Inevitably, reaching common agreement across such a large number of participants was not always easy. Therefore, regional groups of participating departments met on occasion to discuss the progress of the project and any problems or issues that had arisen. If queries arose amongst regional groups that needed central discussion or agreement, these were brought to the steering group, which continued to meet regularly throughout the course of the project. Despite this intricate procedure the possibility remained of there being rather more inconsistencies in procedure and interpretation than in a project of a smaller scale, managed more tightly by a small number of external researchers. This we considered was outweighed by the uniquely collaborative nature of the project.

COVERAGE OF THE PROJECT

The project was designed to monitor all work arising from the Mental Health Act, 1983, which was referred to the 42 departments during the 12 months from April 1985 to March 1986. There are a number of significant implications of this for the conclusions we have been able to draw. Perhaps the most important of these concerns the nature of the target population. We have been able to collect information about all those who were considered for possible detention under the Act whether or not they were subsequently admitted to hospital. Thus we are able to reach conclusions about *who* is being considered for detention and the different rates at which different groups within that population are admitted or receive some other form of care. We are also able to comment on the impact that assessment by an approved social worker (ASW) has on admission rates, as we are able to compare the nature of requests made with the outcomes achieved. The majority of research concerned with people detained under mental health legislation has focused on people who have already been admitted to hospital – those who are often referred to by health and social services professionals as having been *sectioned*, i.e. detained under a section of the Mental Health Act. Retrospective comparisons have been made of those who have been admitted formally compared with those who have become voluntary patients (e.g. Szmuckler, *et al.* 1981), but those assessed and not admitted have not been visible. If one of the underlying aims of the 1983 Act was to clarify and strengthen the role of the approved social worker as an actor in the decision as to whether or not to admit to hospital people with a mental disorder, it is important to know who they *do not* apply to have admitted as well as those for whom an application is made. We refer to an outcome that does not result in hospital admission following assessment as a *diversion*. It is also important to know what happens to those who are not admitted, but whose mental state has obviously been of sufficient concern to lead to someone making a request for an assessment under the Act. We are able to provide information on alternative sources of care given to people who were *not* admitted to hospital.

Because we collected information on all referrals to social workers under the Act, we are able to reflect both on the number of times social workers were required to take action and on the number of people involved in those actions. It is well known that information on hospital admissions overcounts the number of people actually admitted. Our method of data collection enables us to distinguish between the number of referrals and the number of people referred. This is important not only to avoid distorting analysis of who is being considered for action under the mental health legislation, but also in commenting on the extent to which actions follow on from decisions made previously. Many of the people referred to social workers during this period were referred more than once. We term each action taken as an *incident*. The more normally used term *referral* could include more than one incident, for example, a referral for an assessment and a request for a social-circumstances report. These would be separated out in our study in order not to obscure the range and number of actions requested.

The study also included actions other than assessments that could lead to compulsory detention. On the data collection form we specified the major sections of the Act that could lead to a request to a social worker. These included requests for reports to Mental Health Review Tribunals, requests to consider aftercare needs as set out in section 117, and requests for consultations under the provisions for second opinions about consent to treatment (sections 57 and 58). Social worker involvement potentially goes beyond sections such as those that prompted considerable discussion when the Act was passed and we asked social workers to record information about *any* incident of work arising from the Act. In the majority of cases it was clear that the action requested did relate specifically to the Mental Health Act, 1983. Where there was some doubt about whether an action should be included, this was checked out via liaison officers and, if necessary, guidance and clarification notes were issued to all participants. We include in Appendix 1 a more detailed definition of the criteria for inclusion of work in the study.

Since the criteria for inclusion referred to the nature of the work, our coverage of workers included a number of different work locations. Social workers based in generic fieldwork teams, in specialist mental health or crisis-intervention teams, in hospitals and in emergency duty teams were all involved in work arising from the Act and contributed data to the study. Thus as well as different geographical areas with different population structures, we also cover different types of organizational responses to the provision of mental health services and to the statutory duties of social services departments under the Mental Health Act.

DATA COLLECTION AND ANALYSIS

This was not a methodologically complex research project. Rather it was a large scale monitoring exercise that would enable us to obtain an overview of the size, nature, and outcome of work arising from the Act, and to comment on the reality of legislation in action. Thus, having defined the scope of the project, the task was to design a monitoring form capable of being used consistently in a large number of settings, by an even larger number of workers, with limited supervision at the time of completion. A copy of the monitoring form, with its accompanying guidance notes, is included as Appendix 2.

As well as recording information about the person referred, the circumstances in which the referral was made, the action requested, and outcome achieved, the forms were coded to enable us to link different incidents relating to the same person. Details of these codes were retained within the departments concerned so that information about named clients did not leave the departments and confidentiality was retained. Coding also enabled us to establish the number of incidents responded to by each worker, as well as by the different teams and departments represented in the study.

Monitoring forms were duplicated so that one copy could be held in the department in which it was generated, whilst the other copy was sent off for central analysis at Birmingham University. Analysis took place after forms were returned relating to the first 3 months of the period, again after 6 months, and then when data for the full 12-month period had been received. Funds made available by the DHSS enabled the employment of a research assistant to undertake extra checks on the consistency of returns from different authorities and many authorities were asked to complete further checking and amendment of their returns. The frequency and speed of feedback was another unique feature of the way in which the project was undertaken. Large-scale research of this type often gives rise to complaints that, by the time all the data has been fully analysed and written up, the world has moved on, the situation has changed, and the insights derived from the research are no longer relevant. This is a particular complaint of managers and policy makers who have decisions to make on short time scales determined by operational and political imperatives. If research is to have an impact in this environment, it cannot afford to ignore those imperatives and researchers working in operational rather than academic environments are more immediately aware of this. From the start the decision was made to provide regular feedback of results as they emerged in order to respond to the concerns that gave rise to the study and to ensure continuing interest and commitment to it. This was important for the quality and consistency of data input, which depended on individual social workers being willing to fill in monitoring forms throughout the entire period.

We know that this regular feedback resulted in some changes in practice. One department, for example, was amazed at how much work under the legislation was being dealt with by hospital social workers. This led to the movement of mental health specialists into area teams and a corresponding reduction from between 30–40 per cent of work being done by hospital social workers to 5 per cent .

Feedback also proved useful to departments when discussing services with Mental Health Act commissioners and social services inspectors. This may have produced less direct changes during the course of the project. Whilst the decision to provide regular feedback will have contributed to the fact that our final results do not describe what was a static situation during the year in which data was collected, we are not concerned about this. Our aim was not simply to describe and analyse, but to inform policy and practice development in order to ensure that those referred under the mental health legislation receive a fair and helpful response. The fact that our findings have been and continue to be used to review and develop the way in which mental health services are being provided in participating departments, is more important in our eyes than the 'contamination' of our subject of study by the application of interim findings. We also feel that specific organizational changes like the one referred to above would have been easier to achieve than more fundamental changes in the patterns of outcomes of assessment. This core element of our analysis of the way in which the Act has been implemented and the implication of that is unlikely to have been changed dramatically during the course of the project. We do not know whether there has been any change since then, although we have no reason to assume that the picture would look very different 4 years later. Our analysis leads us to conclude that the changes required to make any major impact on the overall experience of recipients of mental health services go well beyond a reorganization of ASWs. However, changes that *are* within the power of agencies charged with implementing the Act can make an impact on outcomes, and it has been our aim in disseminating the results of this project in a variety of ways to assist that process.

In presenting the findings of this project we have had to go beyond analysis of data collected on the monitoring forms in order to provide some context for those findings and also to understand their meanings. In Chapter 2 we start by considering why mental health legislation exists and how it has changed as different views of the appropriate response to mental disorder have achieved prominence. Also in this chapter we consider evidence concerning the place occupied by mental health work within social services departments and what this implies for the ability of such departments to implement the new Act. We develop this theme in Chapter 3 where we consider the intentions, hopes, and expectations of those who campaigned for a change in the law, and the reactions of those who would have to implement it. Chapter 4 sets out our major findings concerning assessments for compulsory detention and the outcomes of those assessments – the core of the 1983 Act. We compare our findings with available information about detention under the 1959 Act (which the 1983 Act revised and replaced) and also provide comparisons between different local authority areas. Chapter 5 contains our findings in relation to other sections of the Act, which provide further insights into the way mental health work is perceived and organized within social services. In Chapter 6 our attention is focused on those people who were assessed by social workers during the year in which we were collecting data, some of whom ended up in hospital and some of whom received some alternative form of care. We compare outcomes for different groups of people and consider other research findings relating to the social context of mental disorder in order to understand the differences we discovered. Our final chapter represents a statement of our conclusions about the circumstances in which mental health legislation is being implemented by social services departments. We consider what this implies for the development of an appropriate resource and skill base that would underpin legislation which was also concerned with rights *to* service.

One final word in the brief introduction to the project. We have noted that the particular strength of this project is in providing a large-scale overview of the way in which the Mental Health Act, 1983 is being implemented. We have not directly included within this study statements from those referred of their experience of being on the receiving end of action under the mental health legislation. We have not talked to caregivers, nor have we talked directly with all those ASWs who completed monitoring forms, or their colleagues in health and social services responsible for managing and planning those services (although we do have some indirect evidence of their views). We think that studies that can provide such an overview are important, not least because of the dearth of evidence of the impact of legislation to which we have already referred. We try to demonstrate in this book that such a study can provide a useful context for the exploration of the perspectives of the variety of actors and those acted on who have contributed to the findings we report here. In taking this perspective our intention is not to deny the validity of hearing directly from recipients and 'actors' what the implementation of the Mental Health Act, 1983 means to them. That is a different study and one that would be important to balance the perspective we offer here. It is too important a study to have been tagged on to a project that has demanded continuing input from a large number of people over a considerable period. Nevertheless we hope that the perspective we do offer here can assist in developing mental health legislation and mental health services that more adequately relate to the rights and needs of people who experience mental disorder.

Chapter 2

THE SOCIAL CONTEXT OF THE 1983 MENTAL HEALTH ACT

Legislation governing the compulsory treatment of people with mental disorder is a response to many different pressures and considerations. Although relatively few people come within its remit, the legislative provisions are a demonstration of our attitudes towards mental illness and health. This chapter reviews the social context of the Mental Health Act, 1983 and identifies key issues that vitally affect the use of compulsory powers.

SECTIONED

What does the use of a section actually mean? Health is a notoriously elusive concept to define, and it is now commonly accepted that few of us are in perfect physical condition. The state of health consists of a wide range of sensations and only a major deviation from this range causes us to define the problem as requiring health-care intervention. In making this decision, numerous cultural and personal factors come into play, each of which is weighed up more or less consciously (see Zola, 1972; McKinlay, 1973; Stimson and Webb, 1975). The point is that we value highly our independence in making these decisions and resist strongly being told what to do: the decision to label a problem as illness, to seek help, what sort of help, and whether to accept what is offered are all part of being an autonomous individual.

If physical health is difficult to define, how much more so is mental health? In an attempt to reach absolute definitions, Jahoda (1958) emphasized such concepts as self-acceptance, integration of personality, autonomy, perception of reality, and environmental mastery. Clearly, all such concepts are utterly dependent

11

on social meaning and interpretation. When, for instance, does single-mindedness become an obsession, or personal autonomy self-aggrandizement? Whose reality must be correctly perceived before we are prepared to say that someone is in touch with it? In the sense that concepts of mental health reflect social values, it is also likely that they reflect the current power relationships in society. This political aspect of mental health is demonstrated by evidence that the fundamental beliefs underlying mental health practice reflect prejudice against both women (Broverman *et al.*, 1970) and black people (Littlewood and Lipsedge, 1982).

How much more important, too, in this most contentious area, are the influences of cultural and personal factors in the decision to label something a problem and to seek help for it? Again, these decisions crucially reflect our freedom, for instance, to go on coping with stress because we value such determination, or to label it a problem and seek help.

Mental health legislation focuses on this area of the definition of mental health and of personal decision-making. At base, the Mental Health Act defines what may be called mental disorder in our society, and under what circumstances the freedom to seek or disregard treatment may be suspended and the individual obliged to accept medical advice. To be sectioned, therefore, means to have no choice in how some piece of behaviour is to be interpreted and called evidence of mental disorder, no choice in whether to seek help and accept treatment – these decisions, and the sense of personal autonomy that they engender, are taken out of your hands.

To be sectioned thus involves being obliged to accept the decisions of others recognized under the legislation – relatives, doctors, social workers, nurses. Who should be recognized as appropriate to oblige people to accept treatment, and the ways in which their powers are defined are essentially political decisions taken by government on behalf of society about the nature of mental illness and the role of certain key groups with expertise in treatment. In this sense, to be sectioned is to experience directly the political force of the state.

Much of the rest of this chapter is devoted to exploring the rationale for the existence of powers to compel people to accept treatment, why some groups have been appointed to exercise these powers, and the consequences of such definitions for the use of compulsory treatment. But first it is necessary to describe briefly those subject to these powers.

THE USE OF COMPULSION

In 1986, the most recent year for which figures are available, 16, 430 of the 237,545 admissions to hospitals for mental illness and mental handicap took place under compulsion. Two points are important to make immediately. First, this figure records admissions and not people: some people will undoubtedly have been admitted on more than one occasion over the year. Figures for readmissions under compulsion are not published by the DHSS, but it is probably a substantial proportion of all compulsory admissions: some indication of this can be derived from a study of people referred to social services for compulsory admission, which found that some 15 per cent were re-referred for the same purpose over a one-year study period (Fisher *et al.*, 1984).

Second, this figure is an underestimate of the number of people dealt with under the provisions of the Mental Health Act, 1983. Estimating the real figure is a complex process. The DHSS figures are taken from the record sheet completed at the time of the patient's admission: the subsequent subjection of that patient to detention under section 2 or 3 is recorded only if the patient is moved to another hospital. The figures hence omit renewals of section 3, detention under section 3 following the expiry of detention under section 2, and the detention of inpatients admitted voluntarily.

We have no figures on renewals but data from the SSRG survey indicated that 31.5 per cent of those detained under section 2 and 68 per cent of those detained under section 3, were in hospital at the time of detention. This would suggest that DHSS data omits to record over 8,000 detentions per annum that largely involve the subsequent detention of patients admitted voluntarily. These represent just under one-third of all detentions.

However, even this corrected figure would not give a true picture of those coming within the framework of the Mental Health Act, 1983, since it fails to take account of all those who are considered for compulsory detention and then are not detained: as we shall later show, for every 7 people detained, 3 are referred for the use of compulsion but not so detained. The upshot of these shortcomings is that it is very difficult to estimate the number of people to whom the Mental Health Act, 1983 applies. Probably, the use of compulsory detention is considered at least 30,000 times per annum and used about 25,000 times.

Returning to DHSS figures, those compulsorily admitted are a minority of patients in mental illness and mental handicap hospitals. In 1986, 7 per cent of all admissions were under the Mental Health Act, 1983. There has been a substantial reduction in the proportion of compulsory admissions from the position in the early 1970s: 10 years before the introduction of the Mental Health Act, 1983, for instance, 15 per cent of all admissions were formal. DHSS figures also give us information on the resident population of mental illness and mental handicap hospitals: in 1985, less than 5 per cent were formally detained.

Just over half the admissions (52 per cent) concerned women, although the proportion of women to men varied considerably according to age (Figure 2.1). While just over one-third of admissions involving people below the age of 25 were women, this proportion rose to 81 per cent of those involving people aged over 85.

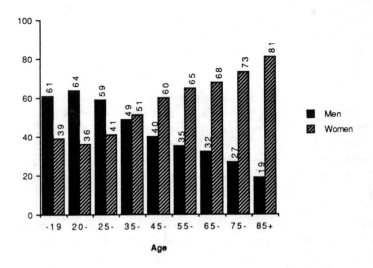

Figure 2.1 Formal admissions: the proportion of women to men by age (1986)

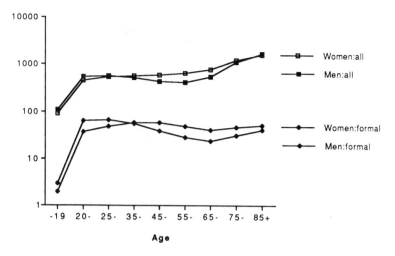

Figure 2.2 Risk of admission per 100,000 population: age by gender

If Figure 2.1 shows the proportion of men and women actually admitted, Figure 2.2 shows the risk of being admitted according to age and gender. In Figure 2.2, the numbers of admissions are calculated as a rate per 100,000 population, giving an indication of the risk of being formally admitted according to age and gender. It can be seen that the risk of formal admission is greater for men up to the age of 35, but that women from age 35 onwards are more likely than men to be admitted under compulsion. However, for both men and women, the risk begins to increase again after the age of 65. The upper set of lines showing rates for all admissions demonstrates that the likelihood of being admitted compulsorily rather than informally is not heavily influenced by age.

Finally, it is worth noting that although the legislation still applies to some people with mental handicap, only 2 per cent (340) detentions involved a person with this diagnosis.

THE RATIONALE FOR MENTAL HEALTH LEGISLATION

Although mental health legislation has a long history, probably the best statement of its rationale was made in 1957 by the Percy Commission, a royal commission, which reviewed the state of mental health legislation and whose recommendations determined the main characteristics of both the 1959 and the 1983 Mental Health Acts. The Commission wrote:

> In our view, individual people who need care because of mental disorder should be able to receive it as far as possible with no more restriction of liberty or legal formality than is applied to people who need care because of other types of illness. But mental disorder has special features which require special measures. Mental disorder makes many patients incapable of protecting themselves or their interests, so that if they are neglected or exploited it may be necessary to have authority to insist on providing them with proper care. In many cases, it affects the patient's judgment so that he does not realize he is ill, and the illness can only be treated against the patient's wishes at that time. In many cases too it affects the patient's behaviour in such a way that it is necessary in the interests of other people or of society to insist on removing him for treatment even if he is unwilling.
>
> (Percy Commission, 1957)

This was a time of intense optimism in medical treatment, engendered partly by the apparent 'success' of chemotherapy. It was also clear that the process of 'certification', a legal process stemming from the 1890 Lunacy Act applying even to voluntary treatment, was a legal intrusion into a field that the Commission firmly claimed for medicine. The implications of this for the interplay of medical, legal, and social viewpoints will be dealt with later. For the moment, we can note that this shift immediately 'civilizes' a law that permits forcible treatment, and places the actions of those carrying out the law in the context of acting for the patient's own good. It is as though having the best interests of the patient at heart is enough to justify therapeutic imposition. This is a powerful shift, reversing much of what the 1890 Lunacy Act stood for and creating an entirely new moral climate around the use of compulsion.

This theme continues into the first of the two principal reasons advanced for having legislation which permits treatment to be imposed on people. It is argued that people may not know that they are ill and thus may be unable to make the decision to seek and accept help. This is clearly an attractive argument, portraying a benevolent state attempting to ensure the best health of its

members. It holds little water, though, since it begs entirely the
question of what *degree* of deviation from health is sufficient to
invoke the power and ignores the fact that the same argument
applies to many physical illnesses.

The second argument, that society has a right to protect itself,
is more straightforward, at least in the sense of having parallels in
other areas of deviance such as crime and having a base in
utilitarian philosophy, which emphasizes the state's responsibility
to ensure the collective wellbeing. The issues this argument raises,
however, about what constitutes behaviour that makes it 'necessary
. . . to insist on removing' the person, take us right to the heart of
the debate about deviance and enforced therapy, and about the
advance of what some have called 'The therapeutic state' (Kittrie
1971; Szasz 1974) and others 'The psychiatric society' (Castel *et al.*,
1982).

What is at issue in the therapeutic state is the tolerance of
deviance and the enthusiasm for 'psychiatricizing' everyday life.
What Kittrie and others object to is how what would otherwise be
regarded as odd, eccentric, or antisocial behaviour comes to be
regarded as an illness and therefore susceptible to therapeutic
intervention, sanctioned by the state in its role as protector of
collective wellbeing. In the context of what Kittrie perceived as a
decreasing range of tolerated behaviour and an increasing
enthusiasm for therapeutic solutions, the danger is that the
threshold for the imposition of compulsory treatment is lowered.

Thus the Percy Commission's lack of precise definition of
behaviour warranting intervention, for the person's own good or
for the protection of society, is extremely problematic. Kittrie's
solution is interesting, and gives a perspective that will inform later
discussion in this chapter on the interplay between medical, legal,
and social viewpoints on compulsory treatment. Kittrie first
invokes Mill's definitions of liberty in opposition to the concept of
intervention for the good of the person:

The principle is, that the sole end for which mankind are
warranted, individually or collectively, interfering with the
liberty of action of any of their number is self-protection. That
the only purpose for which power can be rightfully exercised
over any member of a civilized community, against his will, is to

17

prevent harm to others. His own good, either physical or moral, is not a sufficient warrant. He cannot be rightfully compelled to forbear because it will be better for him to do so, because it will make him happier, because, in the opinion of others, to do so would be wise, even right. These are good reasons for remonstrating with him, but not for compelling him, or visiting him with evil in case he does otherwise. To justify that, the conduct from which it is desired to deter him must be calculated to produce evil in someone else.

(Mill, 1859, quoted in Kittrie, 1971)

Thus Kittrie wrests the moral high ground away from the proponents of medical intervention: merely having the best interests of the person at heart is not a good enough reason for therapeutic intervention. There is a right to remain untreated as long as such illness does not 'produce evil in someone else'.

Kittrie then draws attention to the lack of definition of mental illness. He notes, as have many other commentators, that: 'The degree of illness sufficient to justify society's substitution of the patient's judgment has been neither suggested by the medical profession nor adequately defined in law' (Kittrie, 1971:78). Unlike Szasz, who would solve this issue by abolishing any legally enforceable concept of mental illness, Kittrie's concern is that 'mental illness is not easily defined or determined' (1971:52) and that the duty of the state is to erect clear criteria for the ascription of mental illness warranting compulsory therapeutic intervention which may be verified by reference to observable events. The first four items in his 'Therapeutic Bill of Rights' read:

1. No person shall be compelled to undergo treatment except for the defense of society.
2. Man's innate right to remain free of excessive forms of human modification shall be inviolable.
3. No social sanctions may be invoked unless the person subjected to treatment has demonstrated a clear and present danger through truly harmful behaviour which is immediately forthcoming or has already occurred.
4. No person shall be subjected to involuntary incarceration or treatment on the basis of a finding of a general condition or status alone.

Kittrie thus makes protection the sole defence of compulsory intervention (1) and makes a general plea for tolerance (2). He further specifies that immediate, actual, or threatened dangerousness should be the criterion for the need for protection (3) and that evidence is required rather than merely a professional judgment that (for example) mental disorder is present (4).

Although there are many other strands to Kittrie's argument, particularly on the need for legal safeguards, the virtue of his analysis is that he refuses the rhetorical escape route of liberal indignation and accepts there is a real problem to be solved. In drawing attention to the moral dilemmas of acting 'for the good of the patient', he makes it possible to demystify the medical argument that doctors should simply be trusted to exercise professional judgment in the best interests of the patient, and lays the foundations of clearer, verifiable criteria for the exercise of compulsory powers. Indeed, the criterion of immediate dangerousness became one of the pivots of Gostin's call for reform of the Mental Health Act, 1959 (Gostin, 1975).

Using Kittrie's 'Bill of Rights' as a yardstick, we are left with a highly problematic set of laws governing compulsory treatment in England. The enactment of the Percy Commission recommendations in the 1959 Act, and their continuance in largely unchanged form in the 1983 Act, provides grounds to impose treatment 'if it is necessary for the health or safety of patient or for the protection of other persons' (Mental Health Act, 1983, section 3(2)[c]) and leaves serious moral dilemmas about the right to impose treatment on people for their own good. The 1983 Act's lack of definition of criteria for what constitutes mental disorder or what degree of disorder is sufficient to warrant detention in hospital leaves serious moral issues to professional discretion. It is these dilemmas that patients and their relatives, lawyers, doctors, and social workers are asked to solve.

THE INTERPLAY BETWEEN LEGAL, MEDICAL, AND SOCIAL PERSPECTIVES

The classical description of the development of mental health policy places great emphasis on the relative power of the legal, medical, and social work professions (Jones, 1972). Although this approach has been criticized for its interpretation of all history as

19

humanitarian progress (Baruch and Treacher, 1978; Unsworth, 1979), Jones is surely right in placing the interaction between these three viewpoints at the centre of the debate about the proper role of the state in the exercise of compulsory powers.

It is wrong, though, simply to identify these three perspectives with the legal, medical, and social work professions. Indeed, the legal framework for the use of compulsory powers, from the 1890 Lunacy Acts, through the 1930 Mental Treatment Act and the 1959 and 1983 Mental Health Acts, is better read as the history of changing emphases on the necessity for legal safeguards, for therapeutic intervention without hindrance, and for an appreciation of the social context of mental disorder. None of these emphases belongs exclusively to any one profession. For example, many doctors were active in campaigning during the run-up to the 1983 Act for greater legal clarity about the issue of whether detention permitted forcible treatment. Similarly, the treatment perspective is not the sole preserve of doctors: nurses also are in the forefront of the imposition of treatment and campaigned for recognition of this. An emphasis on the social context includes, rather than opposes, an emphasis on legal safeguards (since the legal context for compulsory treatment is socially constructed): furthermore this emphasis is not restricted to social workers but includes many within the health-care professions who wish to give a greater emphasis to the social context of health. Nor are these concerns the private property of professionals: it is clear that patients' groups and relatives also have views on the relative weight of legal, medical, and social perspectives in the legislation.

This section will therefore analyse the interplay between these three different perspectives, both historically as their varying prominence gives specific character to the legal framework and in the current operation of the compulsory powers under the Mental Health Act, 1983.

The legal perspective seeks to guarantee through specific legal provision that the exercise of compulsory powers reflects principles of natural justice and due process. Kittrie, for example, believes that people about whom medical judgments are made have the right to 'a judicial or other independent hearing, appointed counsel, and an opportunity to confront those testifying about one's past conduct or therapeutic needs' (Kittrie, 1971). In this sense, legalism is the attempt to guarantee social justice

20

through legal provision using the principle that all are equal in the eyes of the law and contrasting the alternative of discretionary justice (Jones *et al.*, 1978). Thus the process of 'certification' under the 1890 Lunacy Act was an attempt to ensure consistency of response through the requirement that all admissions should require evidence to be presented to a magistrate and a duly completed certificate.

Such a process was of course anathema to the members of the Percy Commission, who saw this process as stigmatizing and obstructive of the therapeutic process, preferring instead to lay their trust in the professional integrity of doctors. Doctors, they asserted, are 'better equipped than anyone to diagnose the patient's medical condition, to assess his need for treatment, and to judge the probable effect if treatment is not provided' (Percy Commission, 1957, para. 404). Thus the dispute between legalism and a medical approach is essentially whether it is proper to place such responsibility on a process of judgment that is not subject to lay review and that does not employ verifiable evidence. Is medical judgment above the law?

Many of the critics of the 1959 Act focused on this very point. Bean (1975), for example, points out that the deliberately loose definitions of mental disorder mean that there is no way a psychiatrist's opinion, properly expressed, may be subject to scrutiny – mental disorder is what a psychiatrist said it is. Picking up on this theme, MIND's proposal that admission should be based on 'recent and overt dangerousness' (Gostin, 1975) was an attempt to bring medical discretion under external scrutiny.

This tension between professional judgment and lay review lies at the heart of the operation of the current legislation, and much of the minor rewording of parts of the Act in comparison with its immediate predecessor is an attempt to set limits to discretion. However, a pure legalism also has limits. It is simply impossible to specify in detail legal rules that would encompass all circumstances where the question of compulsion arises, and the traditional value of case law to establish such a body of rules is diminished in mental health, where not only are there very few instances of legal challenge to professional decisions but the law additionally places specific barriers to deter patient litigation (Section 139 of the Mental Health Act, 1983). The danger of legalism is that it is insufficiently flexible to reflect human diversity and tends to replace one set of fallible judgments (those of professionals) with another (those of the judiciary).

Another problem with legalism as a guarantee of welfare is that it pays little heed to questions of resources or of the quality of services. Indeed, it comes as a constant source of disappointment to students of mental health that the Mental Health Act, 1983 has so little to say about mental health services. Although requiring doctors and social workers to consider alternatives to detention, the Mental Health Act, 1983 is silent on what those alternatives should be and what duties there might be to establish them. Although recasting guardianship in a form which is intended to encourage its greater use, work with people at risk of mental disorder in the community requires skills about which the Act is again silent (Fisher, 1988). Although instigating a process by which some detained patients must be assessed for aftercare (Section 117), the Act cannot of itself procure resources to achieve this goal. In fact, the adherents of the legal approach to guaranteeing rights run the risk of damaging the mental health services by diverting attention away from stark resource issues, and away from the majority of patients who are *not* subject to detention.

The arguments for supremacy of the medical perspective in this field have had a considerable battering in the period between the Acts. The Percy Commission was partly inspired by the apparent success of medicine in the early and middle 1950s in reducing the in-patient population. However, the role of chemotherapy in the process of deinstitutionalization was exaggerated: Bott (1976), for example, in a careful analysis of the decline of the resident population, established that the downward trend had in fact begun before the introduction of the drugs which were claimed to be its cause. It seems that what was happening during this era was a greater willingness amongst relatives to resume care of patients and that the role of drugs was to assist, rather than to initiate this process. In any case, the optimism was substantially out of line with the reality of what could be achieved. When Enoch Powell, Minister of Health in 1961, used the downward trends to assert that the next fifteen years would see the elimination of 'by far the greater part of this country's mental hospitals' (quoted in Jones, 1972), he little knew that his successor less than fifteen years later would find that not one hospital had closed and would have to report that 'it is clear that the scope for making progress during the next few years will be very limited' (DHSS, 1975). Clearly, the medical approach was not a panacea for the problems of Britain's mental health services.

This approach was also the subject of far-reaching criticism in terms both of its alleged scientific status and its claim to provide leadership in the care of people with mental disorder. In 1973 a provocative experiment was reported by Rosenhan in which volunteers faked symptoms and fooled psychiatrists into labelling them as mentally ill and admitting them to hospital for treatment (Rosenhan, 1973): whatever the shortcomings of the experiment, its results became popularized and were taken to indicate that the practice of diagnosis was extremely unreliable. Two years later, the Butler Committee, investigating the treatment of people known as psychopaths, had to report to Government that psychiatry had no effective remedies (DHSS, 1975). In 1978, Cocozza and Steadman debunked yet another myth concerning psychiatric expertise when they demonstrated that psychiatrists were unable to distinguish dangerous from non-dangerous patients (Cocozza and Steadman, 1978).

The scientific basis of psychiatry's claim to expertise was under further attack from those who alleged that its judgments were essentially political rather than scientific. In the early 1970s, the substantial publicity given to such cases as those concerning Zhores Medvedev, Natalia Gorbanevskaya, and Leonid Plyusch in the Soviet Union (see Wing, 1978) appeared to support the view that there was no sufficiently strong scientific base to prevent psychiatry being used as a state instrument of control in order to stifle political dissent. If this were true of the Soviet Union, why should this not also be true of the West, and didn't the case of Ezra Pound confirm this?

Lastly, the hospital scandals of the late 1960s and early 1970s (Ely, Farleigh, Whittingham, South Ockenden, Napsbury) seemed to point to the inadequacy of the medical approach in tackling the institutional care of people with mental disorder. Although medical malpractice was rarely a central issue in these scandals, the management role allocated to doctors was clearly not merited in the light of their inability to ensure acceptable standards of care.

What of the social perspective of mental disorder and of the use of compulsory powers? Several threads involving legal, medical, and social concerns are distinguishable. Lawyers were involved in establishing voting rights, medicine was developing a branch known as community psychiatry, and the social work profession, united and integrated in 1971 into local authority structures of government, was beginning to make its voice heard. However, the unifying force around which the social perspectives on compulsory treatment all crystallize concerns the growing awareness that there were alternatives to treatment in a psychiatric hospital and no longer any justification to regard in-patient treatment as the primary means of treating people with mental disorder. This principle, that alternatives to in-patient treatment must be considered, became known as the argument of the 'least restrictive alternative' (LRA) and an exploration of this principle will serve to highlight many of the issues fundamental to an understanding of the context of the use of compulsory powers.

THE LEAST RESTRICTIVE ALTERNATIVE

Originally termed the 'least drastic alternative' or, more elegantly, the 'minimum dislocation from the normal environment' (Bleicher, 1967), the LRA arose from the judgment of Judge Bazelon that St Elizabeth's Hospital in Washington D.C. (ironically the same hospital that was immortalized by Goffman in 'Asylums') was the *most* restrictive environment in which treatment could take place. What was at stake in this judgment was the chronic underfunding of state mental hospitals and the consequent lack of active treatment regimes.

Fuelled by the American Civil Rights Movement, a series of lawsuits in the 1960s and early 70s revealed the failure of the state to provide more than simply custodial care to detained patients. (For a more detailed account of the US litigation, see P. Brown, 1985; Kittrie, 1971; Miller, 1982.) If the state were to be required to provide active treatment in hospitals, the cost would be prohibitive. Thus, in one of those coincidences that seem to be characteristic of mental health policy shifts, treatment outside hospital became both morally and economically preferable.

The concept of the LRA is thus complex. It encompasses the idea that community-based treatment is cheaper than its hospital-based counterpart, an issue of increasing importance as the costs of institutional care became unacceptable to the state (see Scull, 1977; Brown, 1979). It appeals both to libertarians as a further step in reducing the power of the state over the individual and to welfare professionals seeking to replace medical/somatic models of mental disorder with models that give greater weight to social and cultural factors. The wide spread of allegiance to the LRA thus alerts us to conflicting agendas for its implementation.

Imported into the UK by Gostin (1975) and MIND, and reflecting increasing pressure for a return to legalistic safeguards seen as jeopardized by increasing medical discretion, the concept of the LRA surfaced in the 1978 Review of the Mental Health Act, 1959 (Cmnd. 7320) as a proposal to enhance the role of the social worker who makes the application for compulsory detention (the 'Approved Social Worker'). This role was: 'to include a responsibility to satisfy himself that the care and treatment offered is in the least restrictive conditions practicable in the circumstances' (para. 3.12 ii). In this formulation, the concept had already suffered serious transatlantic dilution. A principal objective of the US lawsuits had been to 'make it too expensive to run large mental institutions and to encourage the development of noninstitutional alternatives' (Schwarz, 1974). Clearly, the use in the Review of the phrase 'practicable in the circumstances' was designed to allow for the continuation of the bleak economic prospects for the development of mental health services enunciated in the White Paper 'Better Services for the Mentally Ill' (1975, Cmnd 6233). Rather than underpinning community-based alternatives, the Review seemed expressly to undermine their development by diluting the right to the least restriction of liberty, and started a worrying trend towards the imposition of duties on professional workers without accompanying resources to carry them out.

Second, this phrasing sought to exclude the notion that the ASW (or the patient) might legitimately question the care and treatment being offered – this was to be beyond their remit. Behind this move stood the Royal College of Psychiatists, which objected to any addition to the role of the social worker and maintained that: 'Decisions about the need for compulsory medical care are medical matters, as are decisions relating to the conditions in which patients are treated' (Royal College of Psychiatrists, 1979). This was not just interprofessional blustering. What was at stake was the future agenda for mental health policy in the UK and the extent to which it was to reflect existing, apparently consensual concepts of health and illness or the conflictual atmosphere of transatlantic rights debates. It has been argued earlier that a substantial shift in the moral climate surrounding compulsory psychiatric care was achieved by the translation of detention into the medical arena. Having the best interests of the patient at heart became a justification for intervention.

However, psychiatric care in the general sense also depends on patients accepting the view that their best interests are not always known to themselves, and that those who have care of them may be entrusted to make decisions on their behalf. In this context, the idea that patients should have a degree of control over their treatment and the conditions in which it takes place runs the risk of eroding the very basis of the services – patient compliance.

The White Paper immediately preceding the introduction of the Mental Health Act, 1983 (1981, Cmnd. 8405) revealed further the compromised nature of the LRA: 'The Bill ... provides that ... [the Approved Social Worker] ... must satisfy himself that detention in hospital is the most appropriate means of ensuring that the patient receives the care and treatment he needs' (Cmnd. 8405, para 15). This clarifies beyond doubt that decisions about appropriate care and treatment are the sole province of doctors. While patient and ASW may legally have a say in the circumstances in which care and treatment is given, the precise contents of the medical programme are beyond question. The LRA remained alive, but only on the condition that it did not kick up a fuss: the notion that the LRA recognizes the right of patients to become active partners in decisions affecting their treatment was too radical to survive the transatlantic trip.

The LRA concept finally surfaced in the 1983 Act as a minor rewrite of the section authorizing admission for treatment (section 3) and as a major addition to the role of the social worker as applicant (section 13). After a little attention to the English, the version of the LRA outlined in the 1981 White Paper became: 'the approved social worker must satisfy himself that detention in a hospital is in all the circumstances of the case the most appropriate way of providing the care and medical treatment of which he stands in need (Mental Health Act, 1983, section 13(2)). Again, the addition of the word 'medical' is designed to strengthen the exclusion of the patients' or ASW's right to question the treatment proposals. It is interesting that the parallel duty on doctors occurs only in respect of the treatment section (section 3) where the doctor must state that treatment: 'cannot be provided unless he [the patient] is detained under this section' (section 3(2)(c)).

In its translation into the UK context, the concept of the LRA has thus lost much of its power. It is clearly of limited use either to patients' rights campaigners who want to question the treatment of mentally disordered people, or to those reforming the services who want to develop community-based alternatives. In the continuing interplay between legalism and discretion, the fate of the LRA appeared to cement the position of the medical professionals.

One reason for this is the continued dominance of the hospital as the primary treatment site in the UK. Its pre-eminence is confirmed by the lack of progress in achieving even the limited targets of the 1975 White Paper 'Better Services for the Mentally Ill'. For example, the Audit Commission (1986) has recently shown that in 1985 health service spending accounted for 95.5 per cent of all expenditure on services for people with mental illness: this compares with 97 per cent in 1977 and with the reduction to 87 per cent projected by the 1975 White Paper. Of the health budget in 1984/5, 83 per cent was spent on in-patient services (1986:39). The predominance of health service expenditure on in-patient services is clearly a limiting factor in the development of the sort of community-based services which might make the concept of the LRA feasible. This is underlined by the Audit Commission report that there has been a reduction in available beds between 1974 and 1984 of 25,500, with a corresponding increase of only 9,000 day-hospital and day-centre places (Audit Commission, 1986:17). It is not surprising, therefore, that the proportion of admissions concerning people previously admitted to hospital is also rising – from 67 per cent of the total in 1974 to 72 per cent in 1984 – influenced substantially by the lack of development of community-based facilities to maintain people with mental disorder in the community.

The need to divert expenditure from the in-patient service is further highlighted by the reduction in the numbers of residents in psychiatric hospitals (Table 2.1).

Table 2.1 Resident population in psychiatric hospitals 1974–84

	1974	*1984*
All	90,150	66,050
75+	21,460	23,130
75+ rate/100,000	933	775

This reduction of over 24,000 residents is a substantial achievement simply in numerical terms, although there is disquiet about the lack of knowledge about precisely what has become of these patients (see Audit Commission, 1986). As Table 2.1 shows, however, this reduction has not been uniform. Although the age-specific rate per 100,000 has declined for those age 75+, the overall numbers have increased during the 10-year period, suggesting that the development of community-based services for elderly people with mental disorder has not kept pace with demand. Moreover, the longer the stay in a psychiatric hospital, the more bleak are the psychiatric patient's prospects for a return to the community (Table 2.2).

Table 2.2: Discharges and deaths from psychiatric hospitals in 1984

Duration of stay	*Discharges*	*Deaths*
Less than 2 years	180,086	7,574
2–10 years	2,208	2,944
More than 10 years	1,009	1,394

Put very brutally, the longer the psychiatric patient stays in hospital (and thus grows older), the more likely he or she is to leave hospital through death than through discharge to community-based alternatives.

This brief overview suggests that community-care policies have failed to challenge in any substantial way the dominance of the hospital and have left community-based treatment facilities largely undeveloped. Acute admission facilities are increasingly catering for repeat users of the service. Although there has been a substantial reduction in the resident population, an increasing proportion is aged 75+ (24 per cent in 1974; 35 per cent in 1984) and those who stay in hospital for longer than two years are more likely to die there rather than be discharged into the community. In this context, the social perspective on the use of compulsory powers suffers the severe handicap of resource starvation.

THE SOCIAL PERSPECTIVE ON ALTERNATIVE CARE

Can the social perspective provide a basis for implementing the goal of the Mental Health Act, 1983 of reducing reliance on in-hospital treatment? This section reviews the range of resources that have been investigated as providing an alternative to admission to psychiatric hospital and their relevance to those at risk of detention. The focus here will be predominantly on experimental studies that have evaluated how alternative care compares with hospital care (see Braun *et al.*, 1981; Kiesler, 1982).

Although none of the studies was primarily concerned with people at risk of compulsory admission, the findings are none the less highly relevant to our discussion. Most studies required that those randomly allocated to alternative care were under active consideration of admission to hospital. The population covered is therefore relevant to those at risk of compulsory admission. The studies also emphasize alternative care for people with a diagnosis of schizophrenia; this makes their findings more relevant to those under consideration for formal rather than informal admission. This is because proportionally more people with such a diagnosis are likely to be admitted under compulsion than informally: in 1986, for example, 10 per cent of all admissions but 30 per cent of compulsory admissions concerned people diagnosed as suffering schizophrenia (DHSS, 1987). In the study reported in subsequent chapters, 39 per cent of those referred had a diagnosis of schizophrenia.

Furthermore, there is evidence that those compulsorily admitted differ little in sociodemographic or clinical terms from those admitted informally. Dawson (1972), for example, found no difference in severity of disorder between two matched groups of people one of which was admitted under compulsion; the sole difference of significance was that people compulsorily admitted

29

disagreed that they needed treatment in hospital. Given that there is no clear evidence to distinguish between those admitted formally and those admitted informally, it is unlikely that the alternatives required for each group will be very different.

That most of the studies concern mental health services in the US may also be significant, since it is possible that US psychiatrists are more ready to question the dominance of the hospital mode of treatment. Dick (1981) has accused British psychiatrists of being less innovative than their North American counterparts, and it may be that the traditional conservatism of British psychiatry has favoured the upgrading of the hospital service at the expense of the development of alternatives.

The US term 'deinstitutionalization' covers the prevention of first admissions, readmissions, and the provision of alternatives for long-term in-patients (Bachrach, 1977). In the following discussion, the emphasis is on alternative care for those headed for admission, although the services to be reviewed will also apply to those in hospital when compulsion is proposed. Braun *et al.* (1981) and Kiesler (1982) have reviewed the principal studies and their conclusions provide secure evidence that a wide range of alternative services can be used to achieve at least as good an outcome for the patient as admission to or continued stay in hospital. The resources used have included:

> care at home with or without chemotherapy, aided by visits from public-health nurses
> intensive community treatment, usually at home, involving training in social and daily-living skills in combination with chemotherapy where required
> care in a non-medical group home with non-professional staff
> family-crisis therapy
> hostel care
> day care
> day hospital
> out-patient treatment with supportive individual psychotherapy and family counselling
> (Adapted from Kiesler, 1982 and Braun *et al.*, 1981)

The outcomes for people receiving these forms of alternative care were almost invariably as good as for those treated on an in-patient basis, and were frequently better. Several of the studies were subjected to intensive and detailed cost-benefit analysis with the result that alternative care was generally slightly cheaper and sometimes substantially so.

At first sight these alternative models appear unremarkable. Most involve standard services, skills, and personnel currently available in most parts of the UK. The distinguishing features of these services, however, are not so much their innovation but their intensity, their frequency, and their focus on the support network. For instance, the hostel care was an intensive, therapeutic community with at least two members of staff working at all times; out-patient care involved daily appointments with other additional treatment involving the family; family-crisis therapy involved an average of five office visits, one home visit, and three telephone contacts over a two-and-a-half week period; and so on. This, perhaps, is the single most important lesson to be gained from reviewing these studies – apart from the will to use it, alternative care principally requires *more* of the resources we already have rather than a different type of resource, and requires an emphasis on the support network of the person at risk of admission.

This challenges the often dominant theme in discussion of the use of alternatives under the mental health legislation in this country, namely the lack of alternative *accommodation* for people headed for compulsory admission. Clearly, there will sometimes be occasions where the antagonism towards people from their immediate support network is such as to require them to live elsewhere. There may also be some cases, particularly those involving elderly people, where the risks are sufficient to cause concern (though not to warrant admission) and care in a supervised environment will be required. The research on alternatives suggests, however, that people will be helped more frequently either by working with the existing support network to prevent their ejection, or by creating a support network around people who have none.

This perspective thus emphasizes the social context of mental disorder and draws on sociological understanding of the power of kin and friendship networks. For example, working with networks requires awareness of their power for exclusion. Lemert (1962), in a seminal paper on paranoia, shows how individual behaviour becomes redefined by the immediate network and how this redefinition allows the expulsion of the 'patient'. Similar processes have been observed in families of people with schizophrenia, where a process of 'closure' of the spaces occupied by the 'ill' person has been identified (Scott and Ashworth, 1967). Other studies have shown how the immediate family's ways of relating to some types of people may increase the likelihood of admission (Vaughan and Leff, 1976), how the lack of attention to the fears of the immediate family may result in intolerance of the person's behaviour (Greenley, 1979), or how the support network particularly of people with schizophrenia is overdependent on kin and tends to place people in a passive relationship (Hammer *et al.*, 1978; Pattinson, 1975; Cohen and Sokolovsky, 1978; Tolsdorf, 1976). Conceptual frameworks to understand and work with networks are available to practitioners (see Taylor and Huxley, 1984).

Work that involves increasing the effectiveness of existing networks has been described as 'gathering' (Erickson, 1976). Work with isolated people, many of whom may be elderly, requires a similar appreciation of the power of social networks but completely different intervention, one that Erickson calls 'connecting'. Here the network may be, in Erickson's terminology, 'truncated', that is, small in size and having suffered recent reduction through conflict or loss. The task is to weave a safety net around such people by connecting them to formal support systems (such as welfare agencies) and by creating informal support groups consisting of, for example, neighbour support or self-help groups. In view of the fact that many such people may resist the attempt and behave in ways that may be off-putting or unrewarding to those involved, the further task of the worker is the maintenance of this created support system.

Thus attention to the immediate support network represents a central characteristic of the social perspective and one of the principal methods of securing alternative care. This tension between alternative care as creating better support networks for people at risk of admission or as primarily providing alternative accommodation will be returned to in analysing the resources used to provide alternative care in referrals under the Mental Health Act, 1983.

A second lesson to be learned from these studies is that the alternative care provided for people living in their own homes is, as Stein and Test (1980) describe it, 'assertive', that is, the providers actively involve the people in their own care, pursuing them to prevent dropout, and negotiating pathways for people between the various caring agencies in the community rather than leaving it to those in need of care to work out where to go for help. Again, this makes sense in terms of the fact that many people with mental disorder may be unmotivated to seek help and may deny that help is needed at all. It does raise questions, however, about the translation of this lesson into the UK context. Elsewhere we have commented on the tendency for mental health social work to be marginalized in social services (Fisher *et al.*, 1984) and for substantial proportions of the work arising under the Mental Health Act, 1983 to be regarded as a one-off service (Barnes *et al.*, 1986; Fisher *et al.*, 1987). It is difficult in this context to envisage the substantial perseverance necessary to maintain alternative care being readily available.

Furthermore, the reluctance of some people with mental disorder to receive alternative care is not easily circumvented: the provisions of Guardianship under the Mental Health Act, 1983 are little used (Bowl *et al.*, 1987) and it has been argued that this is principally because they are unworkable in practice (Fisher, 1988). Although some US states have enacted laws permitting compulsory out-patient treatment (Scheid-Cook, 1987), there appears little scope in the UK for compulsory community care of those diverted from hospital admission.

A third lesson from these studies is that alternative care must be provided for long periods if the gains accruing from the avoidance of hospitalization are to be maintained. Three of the studies reported in Braun *et al.* (1981) and Kiesler (1982) were subject to follow-up for a period of between 2 and 5 years. Although outcomes still favoured the non-hospitalized group, the differences were reduced and one study reported no differences at all in terms of psychiatric distress. Clearly, alternative care cannot be half-hearted or short-lived.

Fourth, alternative care in these studies is multidisciplinary and collaborative, both between professionals and between them and the support network. Psychiatrists, psychologists, public health nurses, residential and field social workers, non-professional residential staff, community volunteers, the patients, and their relatives are in collaboration. In several of the studies, the primary means of 'treatment' was the social support of non-medical people, and the primary context was the person's immediate social network: indeed, for two of the studies, the existence of a family network willing to be involved in the person's care was a prerequisite. Alternative care thus requires much more fluid working relationships and a greater willingness to see the person in her or his social context than normally obtains in the current pattern of psychiatric services in the UK. Many different members of the team may be required to take primary responsibility for the person's care, and all members are required to pay more attention to integrating their care with that of the person's primary caring network. It should be noted that none of this diminishes the role of medication as an adjunct to social care: none of the studies excluded those taking medication and many report intensive effort to ensure that it was taken where prescribed. Thus the technical aspects of the medical role are retained but set into the context of the multidisciplinary care necessary to support people at risk of entry to hospital.

In summary, it is clear that the social perspective on alternative care can provide a feasible prospectus for an integrated mental health service. Alternative care clearly provides as good a service as the traditional hospital admission and, in many cases, gives outcomes superior to those available through continued reliance on the hospital as the dominant treatment site. Most alternative care depends on assertive intervention in the social support network available to people, or on creating one, and in terms of individual work focuses primarily on teaching social and daily living skills and on basic support (e.g. financial support and accommodation). Alternative care must also be long-term and multidisciplinary. Successful alternative care does not, therefore, necessarily require innovation, but it does require a substantial increase in the types of resources currently available. Although there are still gaps in our knowledge about matching resources to people's needs, and particularly about services for elderly people, the types of alternative care reviewed are suitable for the majority referred for possible admission under the Mental Health Act, 1983.

ALTERNATIVE CARE, CLINICAL JUDGMENT, AND PSYCHIATRIC CONSERVATISM

If the social perspective on alternative care can provide the basis for implementing the compulsory provisions of the Mental Health Act, 1983, why is it not more widely adopted? One serious weakness in the studies makes such a policy susceptible to dismissal by psychiatric conservatives – namely, the identification of the people who might benefit from alternative care and those who might not. Several of the studies reviewed by Braun *et al.*, (1981) and Kiesler (1982) focused exclusively on people with a diagnosis of schizophrenia between the ages of 18 and 62; some of these further excluded homicidal or suicidal people or those dependent on alcohol or other drugs and required the availability of a family prepared to become involved in treatment (though it should be appreciated that these programs actively sought such involvement from the outset). One of the principal studies excluded those with alcohol dependency or senile dementia (Stein and Test, 1980). Three had no exclusion criteria.

Clearly, the cumulative findings from these studies are most readily applied to those people with a diagnosis of schizophrenia at risk of admission, whose problems do not include violence to self or others or drug dependency, and who retain some form of family or social support network. A problem for practitioners, however, in applying the results reported from these studies is that they are simply too global – that is, they permit a general research finding that a certain set of people destined for admission may be helped equally effectively (and sometimes more effectively) by alternative care, but they do not pinpoint *which* people these are. Thus the research studies have not concerned themselves with decisions of practitioners to use hospital or alternative care. It is simply assumed that the results speak for themselves and that practitioners should make decisions on this basis. As a means of influencing such decisions, particularly those of psychiatric clinicians who may be inherently conservative in their judgment, this is inadequate.

Take for example the thorny problem of whether suicidal behaviour should indicate admission rather than alternative care. Stein and Test make the helpful point that alternative care should not be used for people who are 'imminently suicidal or homicidal'.

However, they then continue:

> care must be taken *not* to hospitalize patients who use self-destructive behaviour as a means of getting help.This represents a very burdensome clinical judgement but one that can be learned and made if the clinician is willing to do so.
>
> (Stein and Test, 1980: 397).

This is a crucial issue. If the social perspective on alternative care is to inform practitioner decisions, surely it must explore operationally *how* to make the distinction between 'genuinely' suicidal people and those threatening self-harm to procure help. The reference to learning by experience is likely to leave the practitioner distinctly uninspired. Similarly, most of the studies report an outcome of hospital admission and, occasionally, of suicide among the group given alternative care. Using the research technique of group comparison, the fate of these individuals is submerged in the overall outcome for those given alternative care. For the practitioner, however, it is precisely the fate of those who do not benefit from alternative care and might need readmission or commit suicide which causes concern and is likely to influence the practitioner towards conservative, safety-first decisions.

This mismatch between the focus of research on the group and of the practitioner on the individual is likely to reduce its impact substantially and, in the UK context, is also likely to be impeded by the dominance of conservative psychiatric thought. This is amply demonstrated in Clare's discussion of exactly the cautious attitude towards dangerous behaviour in prospective patients that the findings from the study by Stein and Test would seek to influence. In rejecting the allegation of excess caution, Clare invokes a *Times* leader praising psychiatric judgment and asserts that *'The Times* most closely approximates to the feelings of the general public on this matter' (Clare, 1976:361).

Such conservatism is bound to provide a sceptical reception for findings that suggest that clinical decisions might be biased in favour of admission. Thus Tantam, writing in the *British Journal of Psychiatry*, doubts the relevance of some of the work in the US to the UK context, asserting: 'that it is not mere prejudice which stops most psychiatrists from reducing their admission rate. There are unanswered questions about who it is safer to admit' (Tantam, 1985:3). Tantam significantly ends his paper with a plea that the 'perils of decarceration' be given equal emphasis with those of institutionalism in clinical practice (1985:4). Thus, this example of how the research on alternative care might influence admissions regarding people showing suicidal behaviour reveals significant obstacles to its implementation. Unless the research on alternatives can provide practitioners with better guidelines than Stein and Test's (1980) appeal to clinical judgment, the individual focus of practitioners and the inherent conservatism of British psychiatry will maintain the status quo.

THE MENTAL HEALTH ACT, 1983 AND SOCIAL SERVICES

The study reported in subsequent chapters concerns the operation of the Mental Health Act, 1983 by social services departments, and the last section of this chapter will consider the capacities of social services to implement the social perspective.

Social services' mental health policy has been noticeable more by its absence than by any other defining characteristic. In the context of central government policy identifying a secondary role for social services in terms of social support for those identified as mentally ill by the health service and, more particularly, those leaving hospital care for community residence, it is perhaps unsurprising that social services' policy is primarily reactive to that of the health service. Thus less than 2 per cent of the expenditure of the 42 authorities in this study was on mental health services (CIPFA, 1987). It is also the case that social services have not in the past given high priority to mental health training, even of those directly concerned in the exercise of compulsory powers under the mental health legislation (see Fisher, 1983).

This lack of policy also fails to take account of the increasing evidence of widespread, but largely unrecognized, psychological distress amongst users of social services. A series of studies using a variety of methods has indicated that the proportion of clients experiencing such problems varies between 47 and 65 per cent (Rickards *et al.*, 1976; Corney and Briscoe, 1977; Huxley and Fitzpatrick, 1984; Isaacs *et al.*, 1986; Cohen and Fisher, 1987). A study by Barnes and Prior of mental health workers in one London borough indicated 'the type of cases which might not be formally classified as mental health cases, but which do fall into this category: depressed mothers, unemployed men and psychogeriatric cases' (1984). Fisher *et al.* (1984) quote one worker in the social services department they studied who asked why they were studying mental health social work – 'We don't do any'. The failure to develop services to cope with this large reservoir of psychological distress is indicative of the absence of a mental *health* policy and of the dominant policy focus on the identified mentally *ill.*

Although the Mental Health Act, 1983 forced explicit attention to be given to some aspects of social services' involvement in mental health work, it has been primarily concerned with training for approved social workers (ASWs). This has sometimes provoked a more general review of mental health policy, but it is currently unclear that this will result in a radical recasting of social services priorities in favour of mental health services.

A further obstacle to the development of appropriate services is the competing demands of other legislation at a time of reducing resources. The shape this kind of pressure gives to the social services' response is well illustrated by the guidance of one social services director following the Mental Health Act, 1983:

It is accepted that the new duties imposed by the Act are likely to increase demand on the department, though the extent of this is not yet known. With present levels of staff resources it will not be possible to absorb this additional workload without some deployment of staff time from other activities. (Because these new responsibilities are in the nature of statutory obligations rather than powers, i.e. we have to do them, some redeployment of staff time is inevitable.) It is possible that additional resources may be provided at a later date though this is by no means certain. In the short term, however, there will be no additional resources either of staff time or support services. . . .

I expect Area Teams to give a high priority to performance of duties arising from the two Acts (Mental Health Act and Criminal Justice Act) while not abandoning altogether high priority work arising from the department's other statutory responsibilities, many of which of course are duties rather than discretionary powers (for example most activities undertaken under child care legislation). Managers in the Area Teams will have to exercise judgment about work to be allocated, deferred, or not allocated, in light of its statutory status and the level of need or risk involved.

(Plank, 1983: paras 5.5 and 5.8)

When prospective ASWs in the same department were asked about the changes they anticipated would follow from the new legislation, most were reasonably positive about the likely impact on the time and space allowed to 'undertake assessments' rather than 'do a section', but they were less optimistic about any positive change in the overall resource and policy context in which they would be working:

> Probably not a lot will change. No increase in establishment or resources. I'll have to fight for space in my job to do this job. I did the training without a reduction in my caseload – I and my work suffered. I wouldn't do that again, I'm still picking up the pieces of what wasn't done.

(Barnes and Prior, 1984:32)

The implications of this reactive stance are far-reaching for the users of the service. For instance, the mother of a son suffering from schizophrenia described how she assessed the severity of her son's state and if she felt he needed to enter hospital she either referred him directly herself, or, if she felt he was likely to need to be in hospital for a longer period, she would ask for a social worker to come to assess for a section. This woman had learned that the only time she received social work intervention was when a compulsory detention was required (example from Carers' Consultation meeting, Birmingham City Council (1987) *Community Care Special Action Project.*

This reactive stance, in which social work intervention occurs at a late stage, also creates a negative climate for effective work. Exploring the prevention of detention in hospital of people referred for assessment, Barnes and Prior (1984) found that most social workers were sceptical about their ability to prevent it at this stage. By the time a referral was made social workers felt it was often too late to adopt a preventive approach. Existing help had often broken down, and some immediate response was required to relieve a difficult and potentially dangerous situation.

The study by Fisher *et al.* (1984) portrays mental health work having to find its place in the interstices created between work with children and work with elderly people. Where there was an overlap between mental health problems and child-care problems or concern about an elderly person's self-care, then there was a greater likelihood that social services input would be more than an one-off response. But even in such cases, the mental health element was not guaranteed to receive continuing attention: where, for instance, concern for the wellbeing of children originated in the mental health problems of the parents, this latter aspect was not usually seen as requiring the social worker's intervention. It was possible, therefore, to close a case when a care order expired regardless of the fact that the mental health problems of parents persisted.

In the case of elderly people, a similar attitude was evidenced by the fact that they were more likely to be allocated to the least qualified members of staff (social work assistants) and more likely to receive material or practical help than counselling and advocacy from qualified workers. Such practical help may be vital in responding to the consequences of impairment caused by mental health problems, but it does not address those problems directly.

Conversely, social workers did not always see the relevance of practical services to assist non-elderly sufferers from mental health problems in dealing with the consequences of their reduced ability to deal with the practicalities of daily living:

> There is little doubt that social workers when actually faced with say, a severely demented but physically fit old lady, would consider the provision of home help and meals-on-wheels. But would these services spring as readily to mind in respect of, say a 40-year-old bachelor who is severely depressed or chronically schizophrenic? The old lady may have an advantage in being eligible also within the category 'elderly', while the bachelor is 'only mentally ill'. Some respondents appeared to believe that these services were not 'readily' available to people who are 'just mentally ill'.
>
> (Fisher *et al.* 1984:37)

The availability of anything more than a minimal service to someone who is 'just mentally ill' could not be guaranteed. Eighty-four per cent of referrals for assessment by a mental welfare officer were dealt with on a one-off basis and 42 per cent of other referrals received during the first 6 months of the study were also 'one-offs'.

In some cases this was regarded as 'appropriate' by the researchers, but 14 per cent of referrals appeared to merit as much priority as some cases on active long-term caseloads.

The intensity of support available in those case that involved continuing contact was also variable. Half received less than 5 contacts during a 3-month review period, and three-quarters less than 10. Contact was usually brief: three-quarters of contacts with those over 65 lasted between 20 minutes and 45 minutes, whilst two-thirds of the under-65s had interviews lasting between 30 minutes and 1 hour.

Fisher *et al.* (1984) also explored social workers' concerns with both the quantity and quality of their input. Workers felt the quality of service was inhibited by inadequacies in their own training and expressed a need for increased therapeutic skills. Their overall description of the skills they felt able to offer stressed personal attributes of caring, perceptiveness and empathy, and concern with individual rights. Most believed they had little more to offer than a lay person with the same attributes.

This negative atmosphere for mental health work is further confirmed by the conflicts and dilemmas experienced by both individual social workers and social work agencies in fulfilling the caring and controlling functions in mental health. As we pointed out at the beginning of this chapter, to be sectioned is to experience directly the political force of the state. The involvement of social work in determining when individual liberty should be overridden in the interests of the health or safety of the person concerned and/or of those with whom he or she is in contact is one such difficult issue. Satyamurti (1979) focuses on the dilemma of the social worker as a state employee caught between a commitment to client self-determination and individual rights to be different, and exercising responsibilities to maintain socially acceptable behaviour. Whilst the powers of social workers have increased:

> Many of those powers and duties involve the exercise of authority, within the framework of a relationship that is ostensibly focused on the good of the client but where there is room for substantial difference of interpretation as to what the good of the client is.
>
> (Satyamurti, 1979:95)

41

A US study of compulsory commitment provides a useful insight into the way in which this conflict is experienced at the professional level. Whilst the US legal and organizational context is different, the concerns of the workers involved will seem very familiar to social workers in the UK:

> 'Shitwork', then, emerged as the product of PET workers {psychiatric emergency team} reviewing their involvement in a case along two distinct dimensions: first, the inability to do anything for a client in a therapeutic sense; secondly the necessity of having to do something to him in a coercive sense.
>
> (Emerson and Pollner, 1975)

Whilst the inability to do anything for a client may be because all therapeutic possibilities have failed, in the context of the low priority accorded to mental health work in SSDs in this country, there is the danger that coercion may be required because of the absence of therapeutic possibilities. Prospective ASWs were asked by Barnes and Prior (1984) whether they had been involved in any specific mental-health activities or initiatives in addition to their formal duties:

> such activities were limited. Six said that they had been involved in no such activities . . . for another of these prospective ASWs, liaison with hospitals and other outside agencies and working with mental health groups were specific elements of her job description. In only the latter case was this type of specialist activity formally a part of the job.
>
> (Barnes and Prior, 1984:20)

This review of the capacity of social services to embody the social perspective on mental health is, then, distinctly disturbing. Social services departments lack resources to cope with the rising tide of demands for social intervention. They have relied almost totally on a reactive policy stance in which mental health services have been developed to respond to the changing face of psychiatric care: the mental health needs of their users have been largely ignored in favour of services for the identified mentally ill. Social work staff lack the training and motivation to take up the mental health component of their work. Such is the inauspicious context in which social workers and social services departments were asked by Parliament to respond to the challenge of the Mental Health Act, 1983 to develop an alternative approach to mental health care.

Chapter 3

GREAT EXPECTATIONS OR MUCH ADO ABOUT NOTHING?

In the previous chapter we have talked about differences between medical, legal, and social perspectives on the definition of mental disorder, on appropriate responses to that disorder, and particularly on when compulsion should be applied. We described how the balance between these perspectives was altered by the 1959 Act, which placed most of the major decisions in the realms of medical judgment.

The tensions between these perspectives remained, however, and the years preceding the 1983 Act saw an intensification of the debate between their proponents. In our view the 1983 Act made only limited concessions to the arguments about the social origins of mental disorder and the arguments put forward by the Civil Rights lobby. In doing so it may even have increased the potential for disagreement between professionals. Nor are we convinced that the Act resolved other concerns raised by the 1959 legislation – over paternalistic guardianship powers, for example, or over the distinction between treatment and assessment sections.

The focus of this chapter is to explore what people none the less expected from the changes embodied in the 1983 Act. Here, we think it is possible to detect three broad views and we describe these before considering the more detailed and precise expectations on which our research may shed light.

Both the British Association of Social Workers (BASW) and MIND were prominent amongst those pressing for change and although the final legislation in many ways seemed to fall short of their aspirations, their leading voices seemed content. Olsen (1984) talked of 'far reaching' changes in the procedures for admission, of 'substantial and fundamental improvements' and suggested that the legislation 'to a lesser or greater extent' embraced all of BASW's proposals. Gostin (1986) saw the Act as 'A landmark in the history of mental health legislation' and as striking a new balance between legalism and welfarism. He emphasized, particularly,the importance of the need for a thorough assessment of appropriate care settings before compulsory detention can be enforced and of the requirement for aftercare to be given.

Such optimism, of course, can be seen as part of a continuing campaign to see that the changes did, as far as possible, have the effect they wished to see. This is perhaps particularly true of the faith both observers pinned on the enhanced role of social workers as a balance to the power of psychiatrists and on the role of the Mental Health Act Commission in ensuring that the new rules and procedures were actually followed. M. Brown (1985), whilst endorsing these views, also revealed another strand of optimism engendered by the Act amongst more general observers – the hope that, despite its limited focus on compulsory detention, the debate and discussion that was stimulated would raise the profile of mental health services generally and in this way lead to their improvement.

Our list of optimists must be extended to include the Government, although they gave clear indications in their white papers and reviews that they saw the changes as perhaps less drastic than other observers and certainly set within the framework of the 1959 Act. Their 1981 White Paper laid emphasis on the achievement of 'improved safeguards for patients' but saw the changes as part of a natural evolution that fitted into the 'high priority' it gave to developing services for mentally ill and mentally handicapped people.

This theme of evolution, of the continuity of policy, is taken up in a different spirit by those more openly disappointed by the failure of the Act to encompass more radical reform. Bean (1987) was a vehement critic who felt that medical opinion had retained its prime position and that the vexed questions surrounding the use of compulsion had been left open. How it is decided, for example, whether mental disorder is 'of a nature and degree' as to merit detention under section 3 or whether the potential degree or frequency of harm to others is sufficient to merit the use of compulsion remained unclear and a medical decision. Nor did he have much faith in social workers providing an adequate check on medical opinion and he argued that only the right of judicial appeal before admission or, in exceptional circumstances, immediately following admission could sustain the individual's rights. He seemed surprised at MIND's acquiescence to the compromise of the Act.

Butler (1985) emphasized the continuing dominance of the spirit of the 1959 Act and saw little promise of change to the broader pattern of mental health care from legislation that was still rooted in institutions and had a central focus on hospital admission and its prevention. An advocate of the possibilities of social work, he was also critical of the attention to securing social work support for some who are formally detained whilst introducing no powers to ensure a quality social work service to the greater number of informal patients. Martin (1984) similarly queried the likely scale of impact of legislation concerning such a small proportion of mentally disordered people, though he saw some hope that the training of a specialist cohort of ASWs might produce a general improvement to services.

Last amongst those expecting little from the legislation, we should perhaps include many doctors. Not all were convinced of the need for change, considering the 1959 Act to work rather well. Some psychiatrists, indeed, thought that it was already too easy for patients to avoid detention. Certainly, evidence since the Act suggests that many psychiatrists and GPs did not really expect the role of social workers to change much and that, for example, when GPs decided someone was to be 'sectioned' and that it should be a section 4, the social worker should simply come out and complete the job (Anon, 1984).

Of course, we have created too clear a distinction between pessimists and optimists and even the Act's most fervent advocates were cautious enough to add riders about the need to provide adequate resources if the changes were to succeed. Resources were also a central concern of a third group of observers – the managers and staff of social services departments who were to implement many of the changes created by the Act. We include them as a third group because theirs was a distinct reaction – one largely of confusion.

Senior managers were perhaps often less concerned with the aims of the Act than how they were to cope with another major piece of legislation being placed on the management agenda so soon after the Criminal Justice Act. There were fears about the potential burden of apparent new demands such as section 117, section 14 reports, and consultations concerning opinions about treatment (under sections 57 and 58), about the possible enhanced use of guardianship and about the greater number of reports that would need to be provided for mental health review tribunals. There were concerns, too, about the precise implications of the new duties for social workers – how, for example, were they to ensure that subjects of possible applications were always interviewed in the appropriate manner?

A major worry was where the resources and expertise to train the required number of approved social workers were to be found, and whether it would be possible to achieve this in time to implement the Act. Managers were also conscious that ambiguity over the Act left them vulnerable to castigation by its most enthusiastic supporters if they appeared cautious in its implementation and yet they had not been given significant new resources to meet that challenge. Indeed, it was the concerns raised within social services departments with the demands placed on their staff that gave rise to their desire to monitor the impact of the Act and hence to this project.

What, then, were the more detailed expectations of the Act's impact, particularly those with direct implications for social services departments, on which the project is able to reflect? Some of the clearest expectations concerned the relative use of the three principal sections covering compulsory detention. There was particularly widespread concern that emergency applications under section 29 were too readily made under the 1959 Act and certainly far more often than had been originally intended. Evidence of abuse and the debate about emergency powers did produce a reduction in the use of section 29 but further reduction was expected to result from both the tightening of the time periods for seeing the subjects of emergency applications and for effecting their admission to hospital and from the clear explanation of urgency expected in the doctor's recommendation. The 1981 White Paper was optimistic that these changes would lead to a restriction in the use of section 4 to 'genuine emergencies' as had been the intention of section 29. Gostin (1986) was amongst those apparently convinced that this tightening of procedures would produce the desired change. Other more sceptical voices (e.g. Edwards and Huxley,1985) suggested that, whilst an initial change might be achieved, there would remain a danger that, over time and with more familiarity with the new procedures, practice might begin to revert to the old pattern.

However, it was not only the use of the emergency section that had changed in the period prior to the Act. There had been a gradual increase in the relative use of section 25, governing detention for up to 28 days for observation, partly perhaps as it had been realized that a longer period of detention was not necessary for psychiatrists to begin an active process of assessment and intervention, and partly reflecting the more dramatic reduction in the use of emergency powers. Both trends should have continued to contribute to the increased relative use of the new section 2, particularly as the new regulations governing consent to and opinions about treatment clarify the position concerning treatment against the client's will, when subject to this section.

Despite increased use of the 28-day power where perhaps a longer period of detention might once have been sought, the reduction in emergency admissions and reduction in overall numbers of compulsory admissions had seen the increased proportional use of section 26, governing detention for treatment. This trend might well have continued, particularly as those once likely to spend longer periods of time in hospital are discharged more quickly and spend more time in the community. These people may often be those well-known to the psychiatric services and if periodically they are seen to need hospital treatment, and compulsory detention is necessary, it would seem likely that they will be admitted under what is now section 3.

The research reported here does not allow us to comment directly on how appropriately the three principal sections of the 1983 Act have been used in individual cases – that would require a finer grained study of the circumstances of those cases than is possible in such a broad monitoring exercise. None the less it does provide the first opportunity to review trends, since the implementation of the legislation, in the relative uses of the different sections across the country. It also provides information on the circumstances in which they were used – including details of who initiated actions under the Act and whether incidents occurred during the normal working day or 'out of hours', and of the people who were subject to action under the Act.

It is also possible using our results and statistics published by the DHSS to explore another clear area of expectation – the impact on admission rates of the enhanced powers of social workers, and particularly the requirement for them to determine that care and treatment takes place in the least restrictive conditions possible. There were not, of course, uniform expectations in this area. Under the 1959 Act the social worker's role was a rather limited one – it appeared to be little more than that of a replacement for an absent relative and doctors often regarded them as having only a procedural role. There were occasions when they felt the medical recommendation was inappropriate and certainly occasions when they would make that clear. In such disagreements, however, the social worker would often feel at a disadvantage with no clearly recognized area of expertise and without the training or confidence to challenge a medical recommendation. The pattern that Christian (1985) describes in her area that an application was almost inevitable once a referral was made was a common one.

The 1983 Act, in contrast, can be seen as creating a distinction between the medical decision about the need for care and treatment and a social decision about who can provide that support and where it should take place. Gostin (1986) and Olsen (1984) clearly expected that a substantially expanded and independent role for social workers in making this judgment would be recognized.

They also saw the requirement for ASWs to have demonstrated knowledge of the legislation, of the nature of disorder and its treatment, and of the context in which it occurs, as important to providing them with some authority to exercise that role, though Olsen is doubtful of this independence and authority being achieved by hospital social workers, whom he sees as still too closely connected with clinical opinion. By implication, Gostin and Olsen seemed to expect more diversion away from hospital care.

The Government signally, placed rather less emphasis on the role of the ASW, not listing it or the emphasis on the search for the least restrictive conditions possible, amongst the main improvements of the Act in its introduction to the 1981 White Paper. Butler (1985) was sceptical about the social worker's role changing markedly, noting that doctors are not under the same pressure to demonstrate 'expertise', and Bean was dismissive of the potential role of social workers who 'have no expertise which qualifies them to do anything except the most simple and basic tasks in the compulsory admission procedure' (Bean, 1980: 215). Fisher, *et al.* (1984) are more positive about the potential role of social workers but feel that the legislation has not done enough to clarify their precise role.

Certainly the dividing line between the roles of the approved social worker and doctor in decisions as to whether treatment needs to take place in hospital is not clear-cut – indeed the possibility of conflict is probably enhanced by the Act. None the less, Christian's more measured response was probably shared by many of her social work colleagues. She recognized that there was potential in the new legislation for the social worker's role in preventing admission to be extended, but that it was unlikely to be realized unless doctors' attitudes changed and unless social workers were provided with the resources more clearly to offer alternatives. Other critics have suggested that substantial diversion from hospital care is only likely to occur with active social-work intervention much earlier in the development of the psychiatric crisis – by the time a request is made for the use of compulsion, it is often too late for effective preventive action (see, for example, Barnes and Prior, 1984).

The chapters that follow will throw some light on these issues. Our results highlight the proportion of referrals for assessment for an application that are deflected into informal admission or alternative care following the assessment of the social worker under different sections, though sadly comparative information for the period before the Act is not available. The comparison of overall admission rates before and after the Act provided by DHSS figures will, however, provide at least an indication of changes in the rate of diversion.

It will not, of course, be possible to comment on the appropriateness of the final outcome of assessment nor to report on any evidence of increased professional disagreement – this again would require a more detailed study of individual cases. Proportions of detentions that social workers felt could have been prevented will be reported, however, as well as the resources that they felt would have been necessary to make those diversions. It will also be possible to see whether particular groups of people in the population are more or less likely than others to be subject to compulsory detention.

50

The results, which afford comparison of differences between local authorities, also permit comment on two other important goals of proponents of the Act – improvements in the quality and the consistency of the support provided to those subject to compulsory powers. Two areas stand out – the variation between regions and local authorities in the use of the different sections and the haphazard levels of aftercare provided. Local variation in the relative use of section 4 was seen as an important indicator of its misuse and something that the new, tighter procedures and the requirement that all local authorities should provide suitably experienced and qualified workers ought to reduce considerably. Our research allows us to comment on the variations in patterns of referral and admission under different sections in authorities with very different geographic and population characteristics and with different organizational structures in the mental health services.

The imposition of a duty on local authorities and health authorities jointly, 'to provide aftercare services until both statutory bodies are satisfied that the person concerned no longer needs them' (Brown, 1983) for those detained under sections 3 or 37, was seen by many observers as potentially a very important step forward (see Gostin, 1986 for example). Anderson-Ford and Halsey (1984) are representative of those who were sceptical of any real changes being initiated by section 117. There is no definition of aftercare services – which could be a simple follow-up visit – and it is left entirely to the authorities' discretion as to when they are to be withdrawn. And what if authorities do not agree about what is to be provided or the client feels they are not receiving adequate support? It is certainly not a strong piece of legislation. Indeed the Government resisted the inclusion of this clause on the basis that other regulations already catered for the provision of aftercare.

Here we detail the reported provision of aftercare under section 117 and examine what special arrangements, if any, authorities have made in response to that section of the legislation.

In a sense, the strengthening of the right to aftercare and a more *consistent* application of key elements of the legislation like section 4 could be seen to represent progress in protecting or enhancing the civil rights of mentally disordered people and their relatives, another important expectation of the Act. Other changes that could be included under this heading are the new power of the nearest relatives to request an ASW assessment for an application and their rights to discharge section 2 patients, although these would have to be balanced against the restriction, on making emergency applications, to the *nearest* relative.

Another area more clearly concerned with patients' rights, however, was the extension of access to Mental Health Review Tribunals. Patients detained for assessment were made eligible for the first time and there are now more frequent opportunities for patients detained for treatment to apply for a hearing. There is also automatic referral to tribunals of those not taking up the opportunity themselves after renewal of detention for treatment and of those detained without a tribunal for 3 years. It was estimated that the number of tribunals would increase from 1,904 in 1980 to about 4,500 a year.

The Government clearly saw increased access to review tribunals as an important safeguard against inappropriate detention, a view shared by Gostin (1983) though other observers such as Peay (1982) and Shapland and Williams (1983) have been more critical of the efficacy of the review system and have expressed doubts about the likely impact of its extension. The role of our study in this respect is simply to document the scale of social work involvement in the tribunal process and so give some assessment of whether the estimates of increased tribunal activity and, indeed, fears within some social services departments about the burdens this would place on them, have proved well founded.

Many observers similarly saw the changes in regulations governing consent to and opinions about treatment as a strengthening of patients' rights, though the Government represented these more as 'clarification'. Certainly, they do not go as far down the road to a multidisciplinary review of the need for compulsory treatment as MIND advocated. Furthermore, whilst they do represent safeguards for patients, they cover only a limited range of treatments and serve equally the needs of hospital staff by making clearer the legal position on when treatment can be given without consent. The balance, of course, between such safeguards and patients' 'rights' to receive treatment when they aren't in a position to consent is always a difficult one and, notwithstanding the exceptions in emergencies, it appears some psychiatrists was not keen on the 'delays' to treatment that can come with these particular increased patient rights (see for example Revill's letter to the *Lancet*, 1982). Again we are unable to comment on the efficacy of these regulations, but can document the extent to which social workers are drawn in to consultations concerning opinions about treatment under sections 57 and 58.

A further expectation of the Act was to remove from its remit certain groups for whom compulsory detention was seen to be inappropriate. The change in terminology from 'subnormality' to 'impairment' was a signal of the Government's intention to remove most people with a mental handicap, from its scope, as the White Paper makes clear. This represented something of a compromise with those, like MENCAP, who wanted them removed from the remit of the legislation altogether. The Royal College of Psychiatrists was amongst those who did not – feeling that there will always be a small minority of people with a mental handicap, but no other disorder, who would at times be so violent or vulnerable as to require hospitalization.

Anderson-Ford and Halsey (1984) doubted whether the change in wording and the need for impairment to be associated with aggressive or irresponsible conduct would in fact succeed in restricting further the imposition of compulsory powers on people with a mental handicap.

There had been a similar unease about the extent to which old people had been subject to compulsory powers and although this is not particularly stressed in the Act or the White Paper, they are one of the groups singled out in the Draft Code of Practice of the Mental Health Act Commission for a 'positive attempt to avoid their compulsory detention' (para.1.25.9).

One particular substitute for the compulsory hospital detention of mentally handicapped and elderly people was seen to be extended use of the guardianship powers. There had been much debate about the efficacy of guardianship powers, which had fallen into relative disuse during the later years of the 1959 Act's jurisdiction. The reduction of the powers of guardianship – bringing them into line with current good practice according to the White Paper – and the removal of age limits on those suffering from psychopathic disorder or mental impairment may well have extended the possibility of its application to mentally handicapped people whilst the Draft Code of Practice emphasizes the need to consider more frequently its use with old people (para. 3.18.2).

Whether Gostin's expectation of a more general use of guardianship as a less restrictive alternative (1986) proves to be justified is likely to be a more open question. He is one of a number of observers who felt that, if one less restrictive alternative is to be provided by care and treatment in community settings whilst retaining an element of compulsion, specific powers would need to be introduced to permit this. One path towards this end would have involved developing guardianship into a broader community care order, as indeed it might almost have become had the amendment proposed in the Commons by Terry Davis been passed, and advocates of this approach must have been disappointed in the limited reforms that were achieved.

Anderson-Ford and Halsey (1984) offered another explanation for the relatively limited use, in the past, of guardianship that remains unaffected by the changes. They saw guardianship as requiring a lot of resources – both residential resources and social work time. This makes it an expensive option – they draw a parallel with juvenile supervision orders – and therefore unlikely to be favoured despite the changes in powers.

Our results will enable us to explore the extent of use of the new guardianship powers, the groups to whom they are applied, and to examine differences in policy and practice that have emerged across the country.

Finally, we should perhaps not overlook the anticipation that the Act would act as a stimulant to improving the quality of services generally. Here Gostin placed emphasis on the potential influence of the cadre of better trained specialist workers, the ASWs, who would have both more knowledge of how services might be improved and also a specialist commitment to promoting their area of work (Crine, 1983). While others were pessimistic about resources being made available, he felt that the new emphasis on prevention would force social services departments to switch resources to mental health work, even where new ones can't be found. Jackson (1983) writing from within a social services department similarly anticipated not a simple change of gear but 'something akin, in fact, to the scale of changes prompted by the 1969 Children and Young Persons' Act, a swift and radical assessment of priorities in social services departments'.

Shapland and Williams (1983), in contrast, saw the Act as largely a lost opportunity concentrating on hospital patients and particularly compulsory patients. They regretted the absence of powers that might provide a more general 'right to treatment', creating *duties* to support the greater majority of mentally disordered people. Anderson-Ford and Halsey (1984) put a similar line of argument, noting that in the United States, despite having a legal process to control formal admission, finding a less restrictive alternative is often not possible because, in the absence of a right to treatment in the community, appropriate resources simply have not been developed.

Clearly it is too early to comment sensibly on the influence of the ASW on the range and quality of mental health provision generally, even were we sure we had the measures of quality to undertake the task. We can, however, reflect on the policy and resource changes authorities in this study have introduced as part of their response to the Act.

Ours, then, is not a complete appraisal of the 1983 Act. There are many aspects of the legislation which may have implications for the welfare of individuals subject to compulsion that we will barely touch upon – for example, the changes to and retention of the role of the nearest relative, the changes to the powers of Mental Health Review Tribunals, and the introduction of section 14 reports. Insight into the *efficacy* of these details of the legislation, comprehensively reviewed by Anderson-Ford and Halsey, will only come from the close scrutiny of individual cases such as that expected by the Mental Health Act Commission. Our research reflects more the concerns of those managing the change brought about by the legislation in social services departments. It may by implication shed some light on these other issues and indeed pose further questions, but its main concern is with a larger scale assessment of the use of the principal sections of the Act, the circumstances in which this takes place, and, importantly, who the people are who are referred for action under our system of compulsory psychiatric care.

Chapter 4

LEGISLATION IN ACTION
The evidence of change

In this chapter we begin to examine what our empirical evidence reveals about the reality of the 1983 Act for social services departments. We consider first the overall pattern of use of the three major sections governing compulsory detention, the impact of the ASW on whether treatment takes place compulsorily in hospital or not, and the resources used in avoiding hospital admission. The analysis indicates some progress in achieving goals concerned with further limiting use of emergency admissions but suggests little extension of the use of less restrictive alternatives than detention in hospital, not least because of resource limitations.

The subsequent section, on differences between local authorities, shows that, whatever greater consistency of practice may have been achieved, significant inconsistencies between authorities remain. It is difficult in the subsequent analysis to attribute many of those inconsistencies to variations in needs between authorities, nor always to clear differences in resource availability or patterns of working. None the less, the results afford some further insight into the circumstances leading to particular patterns and levels of use of compulsory detention and different levels of avoidance of its use.

Chapter 5 examines the application of the mental health legislation to people with mental handicap and the impact of new or significantly altered sections of the Act including those concerned with guardianship and the provision of aftercare. It also considers the effects of the Act on other related areas of social service department policy such as that concerning the deployment of workers in hospital and emergency duty teams and of other specialist workers and the development of further community-based mental health resources.

It is in the following chapter that we explore the social circumstances in which referrals under the Act are made and the influence that characteristics like age, gender, and ethnic background have on the outcome of those referrals.

REQUESTS AND OUTCOMES

We consider first the pattern of *requests* that came to ASWs for an application under one of the three major sections of the Act. It is a pattern that reflects a complex interaction of, amongst other things, the needs of mentally disordered people and their carers, the needs of those making the referrals and the experience of all these parties when similar situations have arisen in the past.

Following an ASW's assessment, not all requests, of course, resulted in compulsory detention. One of the principal concerns of our study was to examine the different *outcomes*, as we shall refer to them in this study, of requests – principally compulsory detention, voluntary treatment in hospital, or the provision of care or treatment within the community.

The pattern of requests does, however, represent the most appropriate starting point for a study of the role of social services departments, and ASWs in particular, in dealing with those aspects of the problems of people with mental disorder that may involve compulsory detention. It tells us what those making the requests wanted and, by and large, expected to happen. As we shall show in the following analysis, those wants and expectations remained paramount in determining whether compulsion was used or not.

There were over 7,000 requests, made to the social services departments in our study, that specifically asked for an assessment for section 2, 3, or 4, at a rate of 45 such requests for every 100,000 population. On half as many occasions again, ASWs were asked to make general or unspecified assessments or to take actions under other sections of the Act, such as section 136, which may have had a similar outcome.

The volume of requests is obviously important because the more requests made the more often compulsory detention is likely to occur. The overall volume of requests seems, however, to have concerned observers less than the proportion of requests for each of the three principal sections.

The SSRG study shows that in 1985–6 nearly three-fifths of requests for one of these sections to be applied were for assessments for section 2, with section 3 and section 4 being responsible for under one-quarter and about one-sixth respectively (Figure 4:1).

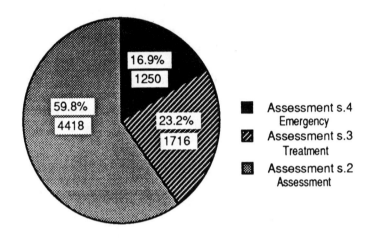

Figure 4.1 Requests for assessment for the three principal sections of the 1983 Act
Source: SSRG 1985–6

Clear comparison with the past is not easy. Most studies have concerned themselves with admissions rather than requests. One study of three community-based teams in a shire county in 1979 did examine requests and revealed a rather different pattern (Fisher *et al.*, 1984). When we compared this with requests for the shire counties in the SSRG study, where there were proportionately more requests for section 4 and less for section 2 than overall, we seemed to have a picture of a dramatic reduction in requests for emergency sections and considerable increases in the relative proportions of both treatment and assessment sections (Table 4.1).

The SSRG study, however, included requests for the compulsory detention of in-patients as well as requests for compulsory ad-

Table 4.1 Requests for use of compulsion – the 1959 and 1983 Acts compared

Data year	1979	1985–6
Source	*Fisher et al.*	*SSRG Shire counties*
		(% total involving each section)
Request		
Assessment for s.25/2 (Assessment)	48.2	57.0
Assessment for s.26/3 (Treatment)	8.9	23.4
Assessment for s.29/4 (Emergency)	42.9	19.6

mission. If we take only requests for *admission* in the SSRG study we see a picture that is more like the 1979 pattern. There is still a switch from the emergency to the treatment section but the fall in proportion of emergency section requests is much less drastic than Table 4.1 suggests. In fact the comparison is a crude one as the 1979 figures do include a small number of requests concerning people in hospital. If these could have been excluded the proportion involving the treatment section would have been lower in the 1979 figures and the proportion of requests for emergency admission slightly higher (Figure 4.2).

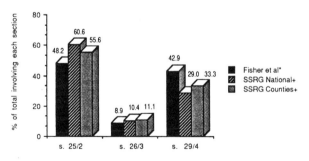

* Includes a small number of requests concerning in-patients.

+ Figures concerning referrals of people out of hospital are drawn from the first six months of the study only.

Figure 4.2 Requests for compulsory admission – the 1959 and 1983 Acts compared

None the less, the overall indication given by this comparison is of a considerable fall in the proportion of requests for the use of the emergency section and a concomitant rise in the proportion of requests for the use of the assessment section with a small proportionate increase in requests for the treatment section . This picture is considerably reinforced when we consider the outcomes of requests, where fortunately a broader picture is available than that given by comparison with one authority, which, as we will show later, leaves us vulnerable to the effects of extreme regional and local variation in the pattern of use of the three sections.

Consider first the comparative use of the three main sections in the SSRG study. Nearly three-fifths of all detentions took place under section 2, over a quarter under section 3, and about 15 per cent under section 4 (Figure. 4.3).

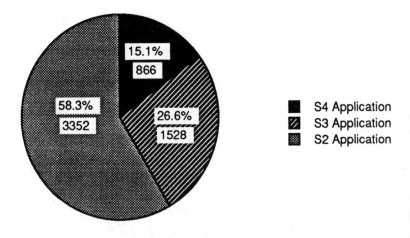

Figure 4.3 Use of the three main sections governing compulsory detention
Source: SSRG 1985–6

Comparing this with the past is again difficult. We have available DHSS data but this principally concerns *admissions* to hospitals and not all occasions when compulsory powers are invoked. In our study there were 5,746 occasions on which the outcome of a request to a social worker was an application for compulsory detention (though there will have been some further occasions when other agents such as the police and courts will have been responsible for the institution of compulsion rather than a social worker's application). Over one-third of these occasions involved a patient already in hospital. Sometimes this involved the transfer of a patient from one section to another but rarely. The majority concerned voluntary patients no longer prepared to accede to voluntary treatment.

The principal official statistics that are available – those on compulsory *admissions* – thus underestimate the overall use of compulsory detention considerably. In this study, for every two people compulsorily admitted, there was another person who was either transferred from one section to another or who entered hospital voluntarily but later, and sometimes only a very short time later, decided they were no longer prepared to stay as a voluntary patient and became subject to compulsory powers.

The comparison in Table 4.2 therefore includes only admissions to hospital from the SSRG study, rather than all outcomes of detention, and this distinction was only available for data covering the first 6 months of the study.

Table 4.2 Comparison of compulsory admissions under the 1959 and 1983 Acts

Data year	1972	1981	1982	1984	1985	1985 SSRG	1986
Assessment s.25/2	35.9	40.6	40.6	55.9	58.7	59.0	63.7
Treatment s.26/3	3.8	10.4	11.6	14.7	15.4	12.3	14.9
Emergency s.29/4	60.3	49.0	47.8	29.4	26.0	28.7	21.3

Source: Unpublished statistics from the Mental Health Enquiry of the DHSS except where indicated.

The comparison none the less shows evidence of one clear achievement following the 1983 Act. Clearly the proportion of emergency admissions has fallen considerably. During the 10-year period 1972 to 1982 there had been a gradual reduction in the proportional use of emergency admissions in favour of admissions for treatment and assessment, but the rate of change had slowed to a standstill by the end of this period. The 1983 Act renewed this shift. Indeed there was a marked fall in the overall proportion of section 4s during the year of our study. This could reflect seasonal variation but the DHSS figures for 1984 to 1986 would rather suggest a continuing trend in the reduction of emergency admissions.

Set in the context of a 5% fall in the total number of formal admissions between 1982 and 1985 we are seeing at the national level a sustained trend of more people being admitted for assessment, slightly more being admitted for treatment, but far fewer being admitted as a result of the use of emergency powers. This should provide comfort to those seeing the previously higher rate of use of section 4 as an indicator of its abuse.

DIVERSION AND AVOIDANCE – THE LEAST RESTRICTIVE ALTERNATIVE IN PRACTICE

We come now to the consideration of another important expectation of the Act – that it might lead to the greater use of less restrictive alternatives than compulsory detention in hospital. Table 4.3 considers the avoidance after assessment by the ASW, of such detention, following a request for sections 2,3, or 4 to be applied.

Table 4.3 Outcomes of assessment for compulsory detention

| Outcome | Request | | |
| | Assessment s.2 | Assessment s.3 | Assessment s.4 |
	%	%	%
Compulsory detention	69.5	85.3	60.3
Remaining in or			
entering hospital			
informally	14.3	8.6	17.6
Alternative care	11.3	3.2	14.3
Other	4.9	2.9	7.8
Totals	4,417(100)	1,716(100)	1,249(100)

Table 4.3 shows that alternative care was most frequently provided following an assessment for section 4. This is perhaps to be expected, given that most section 4 requests will arise at points of extreme crisis, which may pass or diminish in seriousness even within the relatively short period of time within which the ASW's

62

assessment is made. Closer examination of the monitoring returns shows that at times this was the case, though we should not underplay the role of the ASW on occasions in helping the referred client, referral agents, or significant others to see more clearly options open to them other than compulsory detention in hospital. Indeed, this sort of intervention by the ASW was rather more frequent than the mobilization of new resources, such as alternative residential accommodation, or the introduction of new elements into the client's network of care, as we shall see when we consider alternatives used.

This is exemplified, *in extremis*, by the most commonly occurring outcome other than compulsory detention and that was the client entering or remaining in hospital voluntarily. Again, this was sometimes as a result of the ASW's persuasive powers and also sometimes because of a change in the client's attitude to entering hospital or a changing perception, perhaps aided by the ASW's intervention, on the part of care-givers and referral agents of the willingness of the client to enter hospital.

Requests for the use of section 4 also attracted the greatest proportion of 'other' outcomes. Some of these involved referrals that on even cursory investigation by the ASW did not involve people who were mentally disordered. These were often amongst those referred either by casualty departments after attempting suicide or for exhibiting bizarre and often violent behaviour after a bout of heavy drinking. Alternatively, 'other' outcomes may have come about where assessments could not be made or completed because the person referred had died, had been removed into some other form of custody or care, or had simply absconded or could not be found. Occasionally they involved cases where a necessary medical recommendation was not made.

Section 2 requests attracted not altogether different outcomes from those involving section 4, though with more outcomes of compulsory detention – predominantly under section 2 but occasionally under the other sections – and slightly less of each of the remaining outcomes.

Overall, the pattern of response does not suggest that approved social workers were often involved in constructing or reinforcing a pattern of care that offers an alternative to hospital, even if they more often generated or established voluntary compliance with in-patient treatment. In the vast majority of cases where someone requested compulsory detention under section 2, 3, and 4, that is what happened. Only in 10 per cent of all these cases was an alternative to hospital care or treatment provided and in 85 per cent of cases the individual referred entered or remained in hospital. It is hardly surprising in this context that the overall patterns of requests and outcomes were therefore similar.

There were though, 3,206 further cases where an unspecified assessment was requested and where serious consideration of compulsory detention was made, and these do show a different pattern (Figure 4.4). These cases were much more likely, in fact, to be referred by informal sources, the police, or other sources less skilled at detecting mental disorder than the psychiatric or primary-care services that request the vast majority of assessments for sections 2, 3, and 4. Many, thus, may involve situations where the referrer is not sure if the person referred is mentally disordered or not. This would include, for example, requests after an overdose, calls to a neighbour's house because someone was 'acting strange', and calls to deal with apparently berserk prisoners in police custody. Not surprisingly, therefore, over one-quarter result in 'other' outcomes.

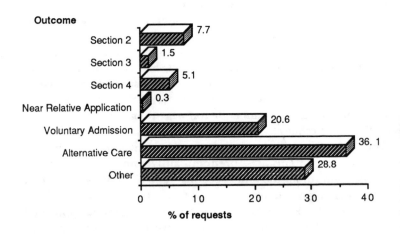

Figure 4.4 Outcomes of unspecified requests for assessment

None the less, these cases were only included in the study if at the time of the request, compulsory detention seemed a real enough possibility to warrant an ASW assessment. Hence, over one-third did result in hospital treatment, although they were a relatively unimportant source of *compulsory* detention – only 8 per cent of all detentions under sections 2, 3, and 4 came about in response to one of these unspecified requests. They were, however, relatively more important for those referral sources perhaps less likely to understand the procedures and practice of compulsory detention. Hence nearly one-quarter of the requests by the police and courts or from informal sources that resulted in detention took the form of a request for assessment that did not specify one of the major sections.

They were also a more important source of emergency admissions – nearly one-fifth followed an unspecified assessment – than detention for treatment or assessment. They therefore had a counter-effect to the greater diversion of section 4 requests in bringing about a close match overall between patterns of requests and outcomes.

A much higher proportion of these requests resulted in alternative care being provided. Clearly those making the referrals, and this was particularly true of the psychiatric services, would tend not to specify a specific outcome of detention when they considered treatment or care outside of hospital might be a likely outcome.

The picture given so far of relatively little avoidance of compulsory detention is therefore tempered a little when the unspecified assessments are included. Table 4.3, which considers all requests for detention under sections 2, 3, and 4, however also tells only part of the story. This is particularly evident when we consider requests for section 3 to be invoked. Here, over 85 per cent of requests result in compulsory detention and only 3 per cent in alternative care but nearly 70 per cent of requests for section 3 concern someone who is already in hospital. Examination of the different responses to requests concerning individuals in and out of hospital reveals this to be a critical determinant of the likelihood of diversion into alternative care (Table 4.4).

Table 4.4 Outcomes compared following requests for sections 2 and 3
concerning people in or out of hospital [+]

Action requested	Compulsory detention	Voluntary admission/ remain Voluntarily	Alternative care	Other	Total
Section 2 (in-patient)	449 (81.9)	69 (12.6)	10[*] (1.8)	20 (3.6)	548
Section 2 (out of hospital)	723 (60.6)	194 (16.3)	201 (16.8)	75 (6.3)	1193
Section 3 (in-patient)	384 (86.8)	39 (8.8)	5 (1.1)	14 (3.2)	442
Section 3 (out of hospital)	159 (77.6)	14 (6.8)	23 (11.2)	9 (4.4)	205

Note. * Includes one outcome of guardianship.
+ Figures based on the first 6 months of the study

There are significant differences in the likelihood of alternative
care being arranged for those people who are already in hospital
as opposed to those outside of hospital at the point of referral.
Indeed, when only those requests to apply section 2 to people
outside hospital are considered, it shows a pattern of significantly
more diversion – similar to that for section 4 requests. To all
intents and purposes, for the one-third of all requests for detention involving in-patients, the notion of the social worker actively
seeking a less restrictive alternative than hospital appears to be a
non-runner. There are, of course, still a significant number of such
requests that end with the patient accepting continuing informal
care. There is also a *prima-facie* case for assuming that if someone
is already in hospital that there may well be greater problems in
establishing an alternative base for treatment and care in the
community. Our study reveals patients referred as in-patients for
section 2 as much more likely to be under 44 years of age and
normally living with either their parents or children than those
referred from the community who more often live alone. It could
therefore be that their principal caring networks are no longer
prepared to tolerate them. People referred as in-patients for
assessments could also be clearly different with regard to the
severity of their illness (though analysis of diagnosis offers nothing
to support this) or could represent a greater risk to themselves and

66

others, than those referred as out-patients. All these factors would render the remarkably high level of compliance with requests for compulsion to be wholly understandable.

On the other hand, it could perhaps be seen as a criticism of hospital care and treatment that so many recipients, many of whom entered hospital voluntarily, no longer wish to stay voluntarily. It would also be of concern if the differences in outcome for in-patients and those referred from outside hospital were due in part to the ASW operating within a hospital setting having less inclination or confidence to check circumstances as thoroughly and form as independent an opinion about the need for continuing hospitalization as they would when dealing with assessments concerning those referred from outside hospital. Certainly, if this were the case, we would have to doubt whether the assessment of the ASW was providing in those circumstances as adequate a safeguard to personal liberty as was hoped in the framing of the legislation.

We would be equally concerned, given the extremely slim likelihood of alternative care being arranged, about the validity of the renewed volition of those in-patients referred for compulsory detention who remain voluntarily. If they are subject to persuasion to remain voluntarily on the basis that there is no alternative, can that be considered to be truly voluntary?

Our intention here is not to criticize the validity of individual psychiatric or ASW decisions. It is rather to highlight, in the light of few new resources, how different practice under the 1983 Act is from the idea of the ASW actively seeking the least restrictive alternative. This is particularly the case when dealing with requests concerning in-patients.

Whether there is more diversion into alternative care under the 1983 Act than previously is very difficult to judge. The evidence of DHSS statistics on formal admissions is that these fell by 9% between 1982 and 1984 but this is in step with the steady fall in numbers of formal admissions that preceded the Act. Furthermore the number of formal admissions actually rose between 1984 and 1985. None the less these figures will have been influenced by important factors other than any change in the social worker's role such as the discharge of more long-term hospital patients into the community and changes in socioeconomic conditions, such as unemployment, that have been linked with mental health. Hence, it may even be that without the influence of the new legislation, more formal detentions may have occurred in this period.

Certainly, on a more positive note, the figures for people referred from outside hospital in our study suggest ASW assessments to have some influence in establishing either compliance with in-patient treatment or in securing some alternative to hospital and it is to those alternatives that we now turn.

RESOURCES USED IN PREVENTING ADMISSION

The emphasis in our review of alternatives to hospital care was on purposive and intensive work oriented towards supporting and reinforcing existing care networks. Whether or not this level of purpose or intensity has often been achieved in recent mental health social work practice is doubtful (Fisher *et al.*, 1984) and our study was not detailed enough to take account of either. None the less, the most important resource used in our study in preventing admissions was social work intervention, and family or neighbourhood support were not far behind (Table 4.5). It is not surprising that psychiatric out-patient services and the help of a community psychiatric nurse also figure in a large proportion of cases, though GPs are more often enlisted – perhaps in a first-line monitoring role.

Other specialized resources, specifically tailored to diverting hospital admission, are less frequently mentioned. This to an extent reflects availability – only two of our authorities, for example, could call upon a multi-agency crisis intervention team, though three had multi-disciplinary NHS teams of an otherwise similar description in at least part of their area and another reported similar *ad hoc* crisis intervention arrangements. Similarly, residential accommodation in the study authorities consisted, predominantly, of group homes or rehabilitation hostels. Only one authority specifically referred to the availability of 'crisis' beds, whilst another made use, not entirely appropriately in its own view, of beds in a Salvation Army hostel for similar purposes.

Indeed, when we examined more closely the actual use of alternative residential accommodation, in nearly two-fifths of the cases, it was mainstream provision for old people and in others provision for the homeless that was used, rather than accommodation specifically oriented to mental health crises. This was true to an even greater degree when we considered the use of day centres and, particularly, of domiciliary services.

Table 4.5 Resources used where hospital care was avoided

	All cases Normal working hours n = 1242	All cases Out of hours n = 462	Section 4 request Normal working hours n = 75	Section 4 request Out of hours n = 83
	[% of cases where alternative care provided]			
Resources used				
Family/ neighbourhood support	42.4	49.1	33.3	50.6
Social work	54.4	45.0	34.7	50.6
GP	39.8	34.2	38.7	36.1
Day centre	8.8	4.3	6.7	2.4
Day hospital	7.9	3.0	2.7	2.4
Domiciliary services	12.6	4.3	9.3	6.0
Alternative residential accommodation	7.6	8.9	10.7	6.0
Psychiatric out-patients	28.5	22.3	32.0	14.5
Community psychiatric nurse	25.3	12.8	22.7	12.0
Crisis-intervention team	6.8	10.8	–	3.6
Voluntary agencies	5.5	5.0	2.7	4.8
Other	14.3	13.9	14.7	9.6
Further cases excluded – no details given	(185)	(132)	(7)	(14)

In cases handled 'out of hours', family and neighbourhood support became the most important resource and most of the other resources were less often called upon – clearly reflecting the greater difficulty of securing access to those services 'out of hours', including the psychiatric services. The diversion of emergency requests shows a not dissimilar pattern though, probably inevitably, fewer resources were drawn into each case and this gives more prominence to the involvement of GPs – who often made the referrals – and the community psychiatric services. Again, the

69

problems of availability 'out of hours' increased the reliance then on social work and family and neighbourhood support. A picture, therefore, emerges of very little diversion into alternative residential accommodation or use of day provision or domiciliary care services that are specifically oriented toward mental health crises – rather that mainstream services were occasionally used, particularly in the substantial minority of referrals that involved old people. Far more important resources in the existing pattern of diversion of hospital requests were resources that facilitate psychiatric care and treatment continuing within the community, the first-line care of family and neighbourhood, and the intervention of social work staff themselves.

This may well have an impact on whose admission into hospital can be prevented. Not only were old people over-represented amongst the people whose admission was prevented with the aid of resources such as residential accommodation and day care but others such as women in full-time care of home and family, people in full-time employment, and black people were noticeably under-represented.

Whether this reflects disadvantage on the part of these groups – it being less likely that they will be provided with this sort of help on appropriate occasions – or simply means that these resources are less relevant in avoiding the need for them to be detained in hospital compulsorily is not clear. Certainly these groups were more adequately represented amongst those for whom the alternative care provided entailed enhanced family and social-work support, but even these showed an over-representation of old people and people living alone. The comparison, though, is inconclusive and the impact of the availability and suitability of alternatives on different subgroups of the population is more clearly highlighted by the consideration of the overall experience of those groups when referred for action under the Act, which we consider in Chapter 6.

Our analysis thus far has shown the relatively small amount of diversion of clients referred for compulsory admission into alternative care. It has also led us to ask questions about the deflection of some of these clients into informal in-patient treatment and about the availability of suitable alternatives. On the other hand it may be, as social workers in one of our study authorities have argued, that in fact the relatively low rates of diversion reflect client needs – that, in fact, hospital treatment is the most appropriate outcome in such a high proportion of cases. We can gain some insight into this by introducing a further consideration – 'potential' diversion of those who did enter or remain in hospital. Table 4.6 shows the proportion of those who were detained formally or who entered or remained in hospital as voluntary patients but who, in the ASW's opinion, could have been kept out of hospital if suitable resources had been available.

Table 4.6 Possible diversion of those entering or remaining in hospital

| | *(% of people detained or entering hospital):* | | | | | |
	Under section 2	Under section 3	Under section 4	As informal patients	After nearest relative appl	All admitted
In-patients*	18.8	14.8	12.5 (1 of 8)	27.6	33.3 (4 of 12)	18.5
People referred* from community	33.2	26.7	34.1	40.2	60.9	34.1
People referred out of hours	*27.3*	*22.7*	*36.5*	*37.5*	*53.3*	*32.4*
All admitted	25.4	18.7	33.5	38.4	46.7	28.5
n =	3,352	1,528	866	2,044	60	7,850

Note *Figures based on 6-months returns except concerning informal patients.

Clearly those referred as in-patients are seen as less likely candidates for further potential diversion, though it is striking that of those remaining in hospital as voluntary patients, ASW's felt over one-quarter need not have done so had suitable resources (often accommodation as we show on p.72) been available. All told, 28.5 per cent of the detentions or admissions in the study were seen as preventable if suitable resources had been available. While this suggests hospital treatment was seen as appropriate in the majority of cases, there remains a substantial minority where the absence of alternative resources was identified as the key factor leading to hospital treatment.

When we examine the resources social workers felt would have helped in preventing these admissions, we see a pattern that is different from the earlier picture of resources used (Table 4.7).

Table 4.7 Resources required as percentage of preventable admissions

	All admissions in normal working hours	All admissions 'out of hours'	Section 4 admissions in normal working hours	Section 4 admissions 'out of hours'	Voluntary admissions in normal working hours	Voluntary admissions 'out of hours'
Family/neighbour support	35.9	40.9	34.6	32.5	36.2	41.9
Social work	34.3	29.2	33.8	28.0	36.6	31.3
G P	31.0	30.9	34.6	27.4	31.2	30.8
Day centre	14.0	12.2	15.0	12.7	16.7	11.5
Day hospital	16.7	13.7	13.5	9.6	14.2	14.1
Domiciliary services	11.4	8.0	13.5	8.3	12.1	4.8
Alternative residential accommodation	34.0	33.2	32.3	24.8	38.7	46.7
Psychiatric out-patients	26.3	28.5	32.3	26.8	22.8	27.8
Community psychiatric nurse	28.0	21.7	31.6	24.2	23.2	20.7
Crisis-intervention team	21.4	26.3	33.8	30.6	18.4	24.7
Voluntary agencies	4.5	5.1	7.5	4.5	6.5	8.4
Other	7.9	6.9	7.5	7.6	7.3	7.9
	n = 1589	*n* = 650	*n* = 133	*n* = 157	*n* = 478	*n* = 227

Family and neighbourhood support is the most mentioned resource and social work support is also important but alternative residential accommodation is the second most frequently mentioned resource. Day centres, day hospitals, and crisis-intervention teams also figure more prominently than they do amongst the resources that are used.

How can this different pattern be explained? Consider the people and situations involved. These exclude people whose admissions could not, in the social worker's view, be prevented and also those for whom alternatives had already been successfully mobilized. They could therefore first include those for whom similar resources to those used in successful prevention, predominantly community psychiatric services, informal support, and the skills of social workers, could have helped prevention but were not available to a sufficient degree. We might expect this to happen in areas where community psychiatric resources are stretched, where social work support is limited because of other demands or to those with only limited sustaining informal networks. None the less those who 'potentially' could have been found alternatives to hospital treatment might well also include those requiring the sorts of help not currently available.

Certainly this might offer a plausible explanation of the different relative importance of day services, and particularly alternative residential accommodation, in the profile of resources required. There was, for example, little evidence in the resources used or in returns on resources from authorities of alternative residential opportunities for those of working age engaged in full-time employment or in full-time care of home and family, suggesting that if time away might be required from a tense family situation, entering hospital may sometimes be the only option. Further credence to this line of argument is given by the profile of people for whom these resources were seen to be required. This reflected the profile of existing use – more people living alone, more older people, etc., – but more of each of the disadvantaged groups were also represented.

The overall impression given is that, by and large, social workers' perceptions of possible prevention inevitably reflect limitations of resources already available, often tailored towards other client group categories such as 'old people' rather than the mental health crisis. Hence amongst the further resources they saw as most important to extending diversion were those of more family support, more social work resources, and further community psychiatric resources that extend the availability of treatment and support within the community. This is certainly in line with the lessons of the literature about building on people's networks rather than dislocating them from those networks during the psychiatric crisis.

None the less social workers did identify considerable numbers of examples that illustrated where this work could be enhanced by extended domiciliary services and day services, for example, oriented towards mental health crises, particularly in working with groups for whom other services do not seem to cater. Furthermore, within the social workers' perceptions, both crisis-intervention teams and specialist residential accommodation

73

were seen as having an important role. It would be easy to see this to some extent as wishful thinking and perhaps an overstatement of the possibilities of prevention, particularly given the limited existing experience of use of these resources. Nevertheless, we think we must give these perceptions some weight, particularly as other research has suggested that social workers are inclined to pragmatism rather than optimism, setting their sights within the constraints of existing resources when asked to speculate about resources needed in 'ideal' circumstances (see, for example, Bowl, 1978).

Nor should the perception that alternative residential accommodation could play such an important role be seen to be out of step with our central argument about alternatives to hospital being largely about working with people's existing networks of support. We have also argued that on occasions it will be necessary for people to seek refuge from the social circumstances contributing to their mental disorder, if only for short periods. When compared with the people studied in the largely American literature on alternatives, which did not focus on involuntary detention, it is likely that the group of people from our study – who had all been detained compulsorily or who were in hospital voluntarily only after their compulsory detention had been actively considered – included a rather higher proportion of those who already had been dislocated or expelled from their informal support network and for whom, therefore, resources like alternative residential accommodation would be more relevant. Presently, when faced with this situation, hospital often is the only recourse. The perception that the provision of alternative residential accommodation might extend the possibilities for keeping people out of hospital is not, then, an unreasonable one and should not be ignored when considering the development of community-based services for mentally disordered people. Nor though, should it be overstated – even if we accept it as *central* to preventing hospital treatment in all the cases in our study in which it was used, or deemed required, we would be talking about less than one-quarter of all actual or potential diversions into alternative care.

Later we consider whether there are any differences in social workers' perceptions of which of the groups of people referred might benefit from alternatives.

TERRITORIAL JUSTICE IN THE APPLICATION OF COMPULSORY DETENTION

As we have argued in Chapter 3, one major concern of pre-reform debate was the inconsistency in the application of compulsory detention across the country. In part this concern echoes that expressed many times in other fields of health and welfare policy about the contradiction between adapting to local needs and circumstances and the maintenance of 'national standards' (see for example, Davies, 1968). Local government and local health authorities are charged with providing services tailored to local needs but this inevitably means similar people in similar circumstances cannot necessarily expect the same service – there may be an element of 'territorial injustice' in service provision. Such differences in expectation may particularly be seen to represent 'injustice' where the deprivation of individual liberty is involved, as in the application of compulsory detention.

Particular attention in this respect was paid during the debate preceding the 1983 Act, to the different levels of use of the 'emergency' admission procedures. These, as we have seen, are used much less often under the new legislation. None the less, while we are sure that some local variation is both inevitable and necessary, we should still have cause to be concerned about extreme variations in the levels of compulsory detention and in the influence of the ASW on its application. Certainly the evidence of our research is that there continue to be enormous variations across the country between regions, between types of authority, and between individual authorities. The variation includes differences in the volume of requests, in the proportions concerning particular sections, and in rates of diversion.

Differences in the levels of requests could, of course, reflect closely differences in levels of need. High levels of requests could come, for example, from areas where high levels of stress and/or rapid progress in the process of transferring *long-term* care of mentally disordered people from hospitals mean there are more people in the community likely to need treatment, perhaps applied compulsorily, in hospital. What is more likely, though not necessarily in contradiction to arguments about need, is that the high levels of requests, overall *and* for particular sections, will reflect relatively high levels of awareness or expectation that hospital treatment will be provided. High levels of requests could contain a large proportion of inappropriate referrals but certainly over quite short periods of time we would expect this effect to be tempered by knowledge of the likely response.

Unless there are significantly high levels of diversion, high levels of requests will mean more people being compulsorily detained in hospital. This, some of the participants in our study have argued, may be a good thing. The people in our study who are subject to these requests are often very ill and in need of treatment and if the professionals involved in each assessment have decided hospital is the appropriate setting then why should we be concerned? Furthermore, occasional periods of active compulsory treatment may both signal a better service and offer more legal protection to a patient than long periods spent in hospital as a voluntary patient without clear appreciation of their legal status.

We cannot of course in this study judge those individual ASW decisions about an appropriate care setting nor the quality of care and treatment offered by hospitals. None the less the study both indicates that ASWs in some areas do judge other settings as being appropriate for treatment in many more instances than others *and* that well over one-quarter of admissions could, in their opinion, have been prevented had other resources been available. This, it seems to us, provides a reasonable case for at least questioning what is happening in areas with high levels of requests and outcomes of detention and low levels of diversion.

Low levels of requests, in contrast, may reflect less need or extensive community based mental health provision. More certainly they will reflect a lower expectation of hospital treatment. This may at first sight appear positive but we hope it is not being too perverse to suggest that it could also reflect a general paucity in mental health provision, a lack of awareness of mental health problems. Even without high diversion rates, low levels of requests will result in lower levels of detention. If this does mean more people receiving poorer care or treatment in the community, then low levels of requests and diversion may also need to be questioned.

The process of examining and interpreting each authority's patterns of requests, detention, and diversion is a task that can only be tackled comprehensively at a local level. That indeed is the intention behind the structure of this particular project as those responsible for the work locally will have a depth of knowledge that we cannot hope to replicate.

We include, however, as Appendix 4, six illustrative examples, compiled with the help of local staff, comprising two of each of the high diversion, average diversion, and low diversion authorities that begin to demonstrate the complex interactions that produce particular local patterns.

Major idiosyncrasies – perhaps the exceptions that make the rules – are difficult to incorporate in any centrally based analysis of local performance. We have, however, looked carefully at local variations for general patterns and in the process examined the validity of at least some of the explanations put forward for their continuing existence. We raise some questions and ideas for individual authorities to consider in their own analyses and draw out some general lessons for our own analysis of the national picture.

The comparisons between 42 authorities are complex ones involving many different indices and are, therefore, difficult to absorb. We make no apology for this and hope the reader will consider that the lessons to be learned make the effort worthwhile.

Appendix 3 presents detailed comparisons of the numbers and rates of particular categories of requests made but, however the comparisons are made, it is first of all clear that there was considerable variation in the volume of requests between the authorities we have studied. Rather more requests were made per 100,000 population in London boroughs overall than in metropolitan districts, which in turn received more requests than the shire counties.

This could, as we have suggested, reflect differences in need, for example, between regions. Arguments are sometimes advanced that the nature of their different populations, or the stress of unemployment, or the pace of change in the economy that affect different parts of the country, will lead to higher numbers of people entering psychiatric hospitals, for example, in the north and the metropolis. This would in turn probably produce a higher level of requests for compulsory detention. There appears to be some support for this thesis in the higher volume of requests in the London boroughs. Comparison of the figures for counties and metropolitan districts, however, shows very little evidence of any such simple regional effect.

There were further significant differences between types of authority in the proportions of those requests that are for the three principal sections. The proportion of requests for emergency admissions in shire counties was significantly higher, for example, than that for metropolitan districts (Figure 4.5) – to the point where there was even a higher rate of requests for section 4 in the counties (7.6 as opposed to 5.4 per 100,000 population) despite their markedly lower *overall* volume of requests.

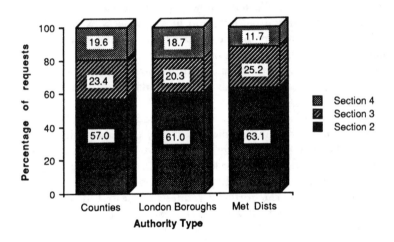

Figure 4.5 Proportion of requests to use the three principal sections: authorities compared

This would seem to lend support to the argument that the greater distances and concomitant difficulties in gaining early access to the psychiatric services in shire counties make it inevitable that there will be a greater proportion of requests for emergency admissions. Such an apparently straightforward geographic explanation can, however, hardly explain the similarly high proportion of section 4 requests in London boroughs. Nor can it explain why, in metropolitan districts, there was such a relatively high proportion of section 3 requests that the rate of requests for this section was almost as high as that of the London boroughs, despite the latter's higher overall volume of requests.

In short, whilst geographic explanations of variation in the patterns of requests to use the three principal sections may contain a grain of truth, in the final analysis they must be seen as too simplistic. In fact, the variation, particularly regarding section 4, is at least as great *between* different London boroughs, or *between* different counties or metropolitan districts, as between different types of authority. This suggests to us that custom and practice, 'policy' if you will, differences between local authorities and their local health service colleagues, is at least as important a factor in shaping differences in the proportion of requests for these sections and quite possibly in determining differences in the volume of requests as well.

Consider first requests to use section 4, as local variation in the use of emergency admission under the 1959 Act was seen as indicative of its abuse. Amongst the shire counties there was considerable variation in the rate of requests for section 4 from 1.0 to 19.7 per 100,000 population. Some of those with lower figures contain several large centres of population and cannot be seen as particularly rural but so did the county with the second highest rate of emergency requests. On the other hand one county in the west, much closer to the archetypal shire county with a dispersed population, was amongst those with the lowest rates of section 4 requests.

There was inevitably some relationship between overall volumes of requests and rates of emergency requests. Arguably more critical, however, was the relative balance between section 4 requests and those for section 2, for which it would be likely to substitute. It was counties with low ratios of section 4 to section 2 requests that by and large achieved low rates of emergency requests, even in one case, despite having the second *highest* overall rate of requests.

This was achieved in a county with a fairly dispersed population and the only possible explanatory factor, evident in the profile of resources that we compiled on each authority, was an impressive commitment to training and information about the intentions of the Act, including an emphasis on what constitutes an 'emergency' under section 4. In turn, it was counties with high ratios of section 4 to section 2 that attracted high rates of emergency requests, including one with several major urban centres, where emergency requests almost equalled those for section 2. One such county with a high rate of emergency requests was actually amongst those with a below average overall rate of requests but at the time of our research had provided little or no training about the Act and had designated almost all their social workers as ASWs.

The pattern in London was similar, with the three boroughs with the highest rates of emergency requests actually having below average overall requests. At the other extreme, three boroughs had less than 4 per cent of requests involving section 4 and over 70 per cent section 2 and it was this contrast, rather than low overall request rates that gave rise to their achieving the lowest rates of emergency request in London. The London pattern is not easily explained – those with relatively high section 4 to section 2 ratios were not ill-served by hospitals (which would probably reduce the number of requests for section 2 concerning in-patients coming to borough social workers), nor in contrast were those with low ratios relatively well provided. Both included boroughs with minimal levels of specialization and training in mental health and those with long established specialist mental health services.

The most extreme differences concerning section 4 involve metropolitan districts. Their exceptionally low rate of requests for emergency admission reflect low section 4 to section 2 ratios in the West Midlands authorities, which also often attract low overall rates of requests. Practice in these authorities is not uniformly well-developed, however, although one authority (with *no* requests for emergency admission during the study period) does have a very detailed mechanism for monitoring each request for admission and a network of mental health specialists in each of its districts. At the other extreme are four northern boroughs with high rates of section 4 requests. Three had high overall levels of requests but again for the other it was the relatively high proportion of section 4 request to section 2 that appeared to be influential.

Examination of the proportion of requests for the three major sections that are for section 3 reveals a more consistent pattern than that governing the other sections, further emphasizing that the differences in the ratio of emergency to assessment admissions across the country should remain an issue for concern.

There is also less variation in the *rate* of requests for section 3 amongst the London boroughs and the counties than for section 4, though still considerable variation, as there is amongst the metropolitan districts. Nor can the five highest rates of section 3

requests be explained as largely resulting from a disproportionately high level of requests concerning in-patients in authorities
serving wider catchments than their own boundaries. Such
arrangements may have offered partial explanations for the
figures achieved in two of these authorities but these five
authorities were also those with amongst the highest rates of
overall requests and often attracted high rates of requests for the
other sections even when in-patient referrals were discounted.
Whether the resultant extreme differences between authorities in
the rate of requests for section 3 can be explained in terms of
differences in the need for compulsion to be applied, rather than
as an artefact of the operation of the services set up to respond to
mental disorder, must remain an open question.

Clearly, what these figures do demonstrate is that simple
explanations of the differences in the use of the different sections
that rest on the 'inevitable' difficulties of rural counties or the
overwhelming effect of large hospitals serving wider catchment
areas, explain too little of the variation in practice. Hence we must
conclude that one major determining factor, if not *the* major
factor, influencing the pattern of requests for assessment for use of
the three major sections are the practices of the relevant health
and social services authorities – the arrangements they make for
liaison between them and the objectives of those arrangements in
dealing with the prospect of compulsory detention. In the local
authority in our study with special arrangements created to allow
the earliest possible assessment by a multidisciplinary crisis-
intervention team and the most clearly articulated commitment to
avoiding compulsory hospitalization, wherever possible, there is
an interesting pattern. Here, a large proportion of requests are in
fact not for specified sections but for more general assessments
early in the development of situations that may lead to the
possibility of hospital treatment, although, as in other authorities,
very few of these assessments do lead to compulsory detention. Of
requests that specify the three principal sections, 86 per cent were
for section 2, 12 per cent for section 3, and only 1.9 per cent for
section 4. Clearly, we cannot comment on whether these were
appropriate requests in individual cases but this is the sort of
pattern that could be expected were section 4 admissions to be
limited to strict emergencies and section 3 to be invoked only as a
last resort involving well-known patients. If it is a desirable pattern,

clearly it is possible for it to be achieved with the appropriate referral arrangements and philosophy.

THE INFLUENCE OF DIVERSION ON LOCAL ADMISSION RATES

There was a similar variation in the proportions of outcomes concerning the three principal sections – though the precise pattern is not exactly the same. This change in the pattern of outcome from that of requests is influenced first by different proportions of requests for assessment where sections 2, 3, and 4 are not specified and more critically by differences between local authorities in levels of 'diversion', following the involvement of the ASW in the assessment process.

Making comparisons between authorities in this respect is not straightforward. We are at one level interested in diversion from any hospital treatment into alternative care but are also interested in levels of compliance with requests for *compulsory* detention or, put inversely, the degree of avoidance of compulsion. This gives us effectively two separate but related indices of *diversion* from hospital and the *avoidance* of compulsion. By the time we break returns down to the individual authority, even over a year, some of the numbers are small, particularly those for section 4 requests and for the diversion into alternative care of people assessed for section 3.

None the less, the analysis does raise some interesting questions. Certainly, there is considerable variation in the levels of diversion and avoidance across the country. Figure 4.6 illustrates the differences between counties, London boroughs, and metropolitan districts in response to section 2 requests. London boroughs were responsible for the highest levels of diversion into alternative care and the highest combined avoidance of formal hospital care whilst metropolitan districts fared poorest on both indices. The effect of this is to bring the rate of *outcomes* of section 2 for the two types of authority much closer together than the rate of requests would suggest was likely. Counties, in contrast, had a much lower rate of requests for section 2 than the metropolitan districts and yet still contrived to avoid formal hospital care for a notably higher proportion of the people referred. The overall effect of the intervention of ASWs on the pattern of outcomes of section 2 compared to requests in the different types of authority is to narrow the gap between the London boroughs and the metropolitan districts but to do only a little to narrow the imbalance between these authorities and the shire counties.

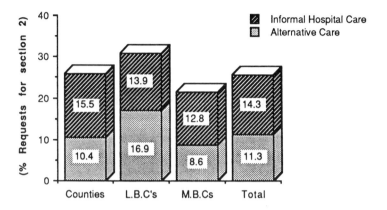

Figure 4.6 Proportions of requests for section 2 deflected into alternative care or informal hospital care

When we consider section 4 requests (Figure 4.7), again London boroughs achieved most diversion and avoidance. Metropolitan districts though, achieved slightly more diversion of these requests than the counties. The overall effect of this will be to slightly reduce the rate of admissions under section 4 in the metropolitan districts further than its comparatively low rate of requests would indicate when compared with the counties. Similarly, the rate of section 4 admissions in London will be brought down, though not enough to prevent its being significantly higher than in the other authorities.

For section 3 requests, London boroughs had again the highest rates of both diversion and avoidance and metropolitan districts the lowest, once more reducing the gap between these two types of authorities when outcomes are considered and leaving counties with clearly the lowest rate of detention.

Overall, these comparisons certainly give the impression of rather more achievement of diversion and avoidance within the London boroughs, where bombardment is highest. Perhaps the higher levels of requests have led to the clearer development of strategies for preventing compulsory detention – necessity being the mother of invention! Or perhaps the higher levels simply indicate a broader range of referrals more often involving cases where hospitalization can be more easily avoided. Yet, particularly if the latter were true, we would expect the metropolitan districts to achieve more diversion and avoidance than the counties and yet they achieve significantly less. Not that we should necessarily place too much emphasis on types of authority for there are significant variations between individual authorities too. In one authority, for example, 41.9 per cent of section 2 requests result in alternative care being provided and in another only 4.2 per cent. The water is further muddied by the differences within authorities between diversion rates for the different sections and by the low numbers sometimes involved.

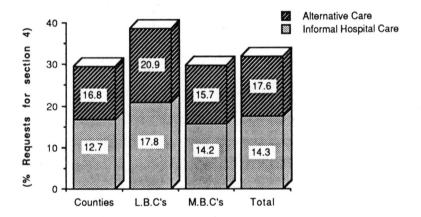

Figure 4.7 Proportions of requests for section 4 deflected into alternative care or informal hospital care

Nevertheless, some authorities stand out for having relatively low rates of diversion, irrespective of the section involved. Not surprisingly three are metropolitan districts and these also have relatively low levels of avoidance by use of informal admission. One has a very low volume of requests and clearly defined procedures for carefully monitoring all admissions, so it may be, therefore, that requests are restricted largely to those where the possibilities of alternative forms of care have already been carefully considered. Another, in contrast, has the second highest overall volume of requests, and now the highest level of outcomes of compulsory detention. One county has similarly low levels of all-round diversion though a higher incidence of avoidance. No other authorities have uniformly low levels of diversion or avoidance. Three authorities though do divert very few section 2 referrals into alternative care. Similarly, some authorities have little diversion of section 4s or section 3s but the numbers involved are small in relation to the overall pattern and one or two different outcomes would dramatically alter the picture.

At the other extreme, we have authorities that stand out for high levels of diversion. One London borough is signally successful at overall diversion, despite a low bombardment rate. This was not a borough that had devoted exceptional resources to mental health services but it did monitor every 'section' centrally and there were monthly meetings oriented to producing a consistent departmental response to requests for detention. Two further boroughs and one county are also very successful at diverting section 2 referrals, though they have either very few section 3 and 4 requests or only average levels of diversion. All three also achieve relatively high levels of avoidance through informal admission. Again there is no simple relationship with bombardment rates as two of these authorities have amongst the highest rates but the other a below average request rate. Though again, none had access to exceptional levels of community-based resources, these three authorities do stand out for their commitment to training and developing detailed guidance on expected responses under the Act and/or a clearly articulated commitment to community psychiatric treatment.

Three further London boroughs and one metropolitan district divert relatively high proportions of section 4s but all achieve little diversion of requests for the other sections and only average or little avoidance of compulsion by means of redirection into informal admission. All have above average bombardment rates for section 4 referrals and two special crisis-intervention arrangements for assessing such emergencies.

Overall what then does this examination of the performances of different local authorities tell us? The first point to note is the relationship between diversion into alternative care and avoidance of compulsion by redirection into informal admission. There is not a straightforward relationship, and there are authorities where there is little diversion but considerable avoidance and vice versa, but, as the comparison between types of authority indicated, so the analysis of individual authorities reinforces that more often than not, the two occur together. Hence, in authorities where they are successful at diverting into alternative care, so social work intervention also more often results in the people referred entering or staying in hospital informally.

But why do some authorities achieve more diversion and avoidance of formal admission than others? There are several contributors to the dynamic that creates the level of diversion in particular authorities including: the level and appropriateness of requests made, the characteristics of the populations, relationships between local authorities and the local health services, and the values, knowledge, and skills that guide the ASWs' assessments and decision-making and the resources available to them. The interaction of these factors in each individual authority is something we cannot fully unravel in this study. It is something, as we have argued, best answered by the authorities themselves, from their own analysis and with their own more finely tuned awareness of their own local circumstances. Indeed, several authorities have already used the data supplied by the study to ask exactly these questions of their own authority's performance when compared with national figures.

We can, however, offer some pointers from our overall analysis that highlight the complexity of the issues involved. It can be argued, for example, that if more requests are made for assessments for hospital care where some community-based care is more appropriate, there will be more scope for diversion and levels of diversion might be expected to be higher. In contrast, low rates of referral and diversion might be expected where referral arrangements were clearer and criteria as to what is an appropriate referral more clearly agreed between key professionals. This might be seen as good practice.

It is an argument that can be seen to have particular merit when we consider referrals for assessment for section 3 when we would expect it to be more likely that the referred person and both their disorder *and* social circumstances would be known to the professionals involved. It is a less tenable argument when we consider requests for section 2 and 4 where it is much more likely that an immediate crisis is involved. Then the referrer, and medical opinion, when the referral does not come from a doctor, will see an apparent need for compulsory hospital treatment but not have the full grasp of particularly the social circumstances and possibilities of alternative treatment that the ASWs' independent assessment should reveal.

In fact, there is no clear relationship between bombardment rates and diversion. True the London boroughs with their higher rates of bombardment generally achieved more diversion but even at this level of analysis by authority type we found exceptions to any straightforward relationship. More significantly, once we extend the analysis to individual authorities, the argument that it is authorities with high levels of requests that achieve most diversion falls apart. Authorities with both high and low levels of bombardment figure amongst both those who do achieve significant levels of diversion and those who do not. In fact, on balance it is perhaps the lower bombardment authorities who achieve most diversion and vice versa.

Of course, irrespective of levels of bombardment, the argument could still hold that areas with high levels of diversion are those with low proportions of referrals from the sources most likely to be well informed or perhaps persuasive – psychiatric services – rather than other major sources such as the police and GPs. Certainly, as Figure 4.8 suggests, rather fewer referrals from this source overall result in alternative care being provided. However, when we checked the eight authorities that were respectively the four with the highest and lowest levels of diversion, there was no clear relationship between sources of referral and diversion. Only one of the low diversion authorities had a noticeably higher proportion of referrals from the psychiatric services and then only for section 2 requests. In two of the high diversion authorities we did find the expected relationship but in another there was actually a larger proportion of requests from the psychiatric services. It was the other authority in the latter group, however, that produces the most telling result. It does have a slightly lower proportion of its requests, for example, for section 2 assessments, emanating from the psychiatric services, but these particular requests actually led to greater than average diversion into alternative care and this was indicative of a general pattern. That is that in these authorities, the overall patterns of diversion exerted a stronger influence than the effect of sources of referral. Hence, in the authorities where most diversion took place, it was not that more requests came from the sources that more often than others led to alternative care, but rather that in those authorities even requests from those sources that overall generated most outcomes of detention were more likely to be diverted into alternative care. The tendency or ability of ASWs to find alternative outcomes overrode the influence of the referral source.

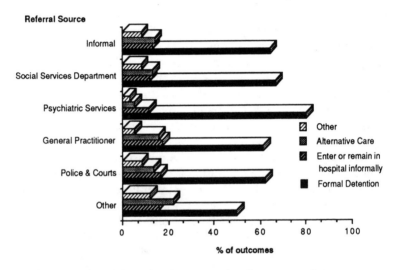

Figure 4.8 The relationship between referral sources and outcomes (requests for sections 2, 3, or 4)

The quality of referrals, inasmuch as we can equate this with proportions of referrals coming from more authoritative sources, may perhaps influence levels of diversion but does not seem too critical. Are *resources*, then, the critical influence? Comparing resources between authorities is difficult but certainly there was little indication in the evidence gathered in our study that authorities with high rates of diversion had access to exceptional levels or kinds of resources, with the exception of two authorities with high levels of section 4 diversion where there were special crisis intervention arrangements to deal with such emergencies.

We are not here intending to argue that resources shortages do not place restrictions on levels of diversion. It is apparent that they do, for example, in the relatively high proportion of admissions social workers saw as preventable. Rather, we are arguing that even in areas where levels of requests were not so high as to suggest large numbers of inappropriate referrals and where there were not significantly different resources for this work, relatively high levels of diversion do seem to have been achieved.

Nor could we find any clear evidence that there was one organizational model that stood out as under-pinning high levels of diversion. Although, as we will show in Chapter 5 where we explore organizational issues in more depth, there does appear to be some relationship between the number and deployment of ASWs and outcomes, high and low diversion authorities encompassed a range of different organizational relationships. For example, the high-diversion authorities A and B, described in some detail in Appendix 4, have very contrasting arrangements.

Differences between local authorities in their assessment of 'potential' diversion offer no fundamental insights into the reasons behind existing diversion rates but neither do they contradict our central thesis that rates of request and diversion are shaped predominantly by local policy choices or their absence. Five authorities registered low potential diversion across the board. Perhaps surprisingly, four of these had relatively high rates of detention. The fifth had a slightly below average rate of outcome of formal detention. In none of these authorities was there much existing diversion into alternative care (although one of them had considerable diversion of section 4s, its overall rates of diversion were low). This suggests to us either a very pessimistic view of diversion by local ASWs and/or satisfaction with the decisions and the policies framing them that led to existing high rates of detention.

Neither, however, were the authorities in which most further prevention was seen as possible, amongst those responsible for most existing diversion. Of the three showing most optimism about further prevention, one county did have a low rate of formal detention but this was determined by low rates of requests rather than by any exceptional success at diversion. Another, a London borough, had average rates of formal detention and diversion and the third, a metropolitan district, an above-average rate of detention and only average current diversion.

With one or two exceptions, those already achieving the higher levels of diversion fell in the middle – neither suffering from the pessimism of the spirit nor satisfaction at their current levels of achievement that might be expected to mark out those authorities anticipating little further prevention nor seeing the greatest scope for further prevention.

Overall then, existing levels of diversion do vary between authorities, though in most cases, given the relatively low average level of diversion, not enough to prevent the level of demand, or requests, being the strongest influence on the final pattern of admissions. None the less the variation, in relation to sections 2 and 4 particularly, is such as to suggest that the intervention of the ASW is having a differential impact on the likelihood of the person referred entering hospital or becoming subject to compulsory detention. In other social work contexts such 'territorial injustice' has been both deplored and yet seen as an inevitable consequence of the need of local authorities to fine tune their services to reflect the particular local set of needs and resources available. In the context of legislation setting up the ASWs' assessment as a quasi-legal defender of rights it is perhaps more disturbing.

It would, however, be simplistic to say that high diversion authorities were always those with the most highly developed or sophisticated mental health services. Our own view is that the complexity of the factors influencing both the rates of requests for the different sections and diversion render both suspect as indicators *on their own* of a 'good' or 'bad' authority.

None the less the extreme variation reinforces our feeling that authorities should compare their own patterns of referral and diversion with the national picture and consider whether their own performance is satisfactory. Just as some authorities appeared to have reduced requests for emergency admission to a very low level, some authorities did achieve high levels of diversion and if that is desirable then it can be achieved. The most consistently significant factor in these authorities seems to be the degree of commitment to ensuring that the social perspective on where treatment for mental disorder should take place is acknowledged as the legislation intended. Hence higher diversion authorities are often characterized by their commitment to ASW training, to formulating clear guidance on how the legislation was to be implemented, and to evolving working relationships with local health services that acknowledged the appropriate competence of all the professionals involved in decisions about compulsory treatment.

Chapter 5

ONE STEP FORWARD. . . .

Many of the expectations of the 1983 Act that we considered in Chapter 3 concerned the impact of the ASWs', assessments on the patterns of compulsory admission, both nationwide and within individual authorities, that we have just explored. There were, however, a number of other important changes that some observers at least hoped would take place following the passage of the Act. We consider first the implications of the Act for people with a mental handicap, then examine the use of its new or significantly altered sections, and finally consider other areas of social service department practice, like involvement with section 136 and the precise location of ASWs within departmental structures that were the subject of some debate prior to 1983 but not directly subject to fresh legislation. Overall, this analysis serves to illustrate the inconsistencies in both the legislative definition of the approved social worker's role and in their deployment at the local level that signal the ambiguity that remains about the part they have to play in the management of the care and treatment of mentally disordered people.

THE MENTAL HEALTH ACT AND MENTAL HANDICAP

There is a higher degree of consensus about the role of social services departments in providing services for people with mental handicap and the philosophy that should underpin that role than there is in relation to people with mental disorder. One consequence is a general acceptance that it is rarely appropriate to apply the mental health legislation to people with a mental handicap. The Mental Health Act, 1983 does not mention the words 'mental handicap'. Section 1 'Application of Act' refers to mental impairment and severe mental impairment and makes it clear that impairment *per se* should not lead to reception into hospital, or to care or treatment under the Act:

> Severe mental impairment' means a state of arrested or incomplete development of mind which includes severe impairment of intelligence and social functioning *and* {our emphasis} is associated with abnormally aggressive or seriously irresponsible conduct on the part of the person concerned and 'severely mentally impaired' shall be construed accordingly.
>
> (Section 1 (2))

The definition of mental impairment differs only in the absence of the word 'severe' and its replacement by 'significant' (i.e. significant impairment of intelligence). In the original Draft Code of Practice produced by the Mental Health Act Commission (1985), the lack of a tight definition of the characteristics of people with a mental handicap was considered to be an ambiguous virtue.

> It can be argued that excessive zeal in generating tight operational definitions of these characteristics is unwarranted and could lead to an inability to detain where clinical judgement would have considered detention to be appropriate. On the other hand, the danger exists that mentally handicapped people could become detained under the Act on grounds which are not explicit and which may be questionable both ethically and legally. This is particularly worrying in view of the vulnerability of mentally handicapped people to decisions being taken about their status without their active and informed involvement.
>
> (para. 1.10.3)

The latter danger is considered to be sufficiently worrying for the commission to attempt its own definition of (i) 'Abnormally aggressive' and (ii) 'Seriously irresponsible conduct' (para. 1.10.4).

> (i) 'Behaviour which is mostly unpredictable and severe, causing damage or distress and occurring either recently or persistently or with excessive severity. Examples are:

damaging others by physical acts, throwing objects to cause damage to others.'

(ii) 'Behaviour which frequently constitutes a serious or potentially serious danger, where the person concerned does not show appropriate regard to its consequences. Examples are: absconding, arson, life-endangering self-neglect.'

The overall concern of the Commission as expressed in the Draft Code was that questions of legal and civil rights in relation to people with a mental handicap are particularly sensitive and that this implies even greater responsibility on the part of professionals and managers in the health and social services to ensure professional standards in treatment and care. By and large, people with a mental handicap should not be liable to the compulsory powers of detention, and where they are, this should usually be as a result of some additional disability.

In fact it is rare for people with a diagnosis of mental handicap to be referred for action under the 1983 Act. Our study included 88 incidents concerning 72 people in 42 local authority areas during the course of a year, including 10 in one authority. Another way of looking at that is that an ASW could expect to be asked to assess someone with a mental handicap once in 25 years.

This can be seen as a positive indication of a restricted use of the legislation in relation to people with a mental handicap. However, the severity of the circumstances implied by the Commission's definitions would suggest that the fact that over 23 per cent of referrals of people with a mental handicap were of people previously unknown to the department might be a matter for concern.

The majority of people with a mental handicap who were referred were young: 41 were under 35 and only one woman was over 65. There were more men than women: 42 compared with 28, and this stands in contrast with the gender distribution amongst all those referred for action. This is probably a reflection of the age distribution as there were more men than women amongst the younger age groups of those referred, although it may also reflect the physically violent and aggressive behaviour that the Commission suggested could justify action under the Act. Fifty-nine people were single and only 6 were married (5 of them women). The majority were living either with their parents (26), or in residential units provided either by the NHS or less frequently, by the social services department or private or voluntary agencies (24). Eight were living alone. Seventy-four per cent were unemployed and a further 19 per cent had an employment status categorized as 'other' (registered disabled, ATC trainee, etc.). All but 2 were white.

This is the sort of picture one would expect: a group who are still largely dependent on their family of origin or the statutory agencies for support, few of whom have any status within the productive or reproductive institutions of society. Although the numbers were small, the fact that four times as many were living in National Health Service units compared with social service residential units, suggests that they may have had particularly severe problems, which may have meant that they were not among the earliest groups to be discharged from hospital under community care schemes.

The pattern of requests for action was very different from that of the population as a whole. Of a total of 65 requests asking for some form of assessment 18 were for guardianship, 16 for assessment under section 3, 12 for assessment under section 2, and 9 for assessment under section 4. There were 8 'not specified' assessment requests and one request under section 136.

Of the requests that might have led to compulsory detention, 26 (40 per cent) did result in such a detention, 7 (10.8 per cent) resulted in informal admission or continuing informal patient status, 14 (21.5 per cent) resulted in an application for guardianship, and in 12 cases (18.5 per cent) some form of alternative care was found.

The most obvious difference was in the use of guardianship. The Draft Code of Practice suggested that guardianship might be particularly appropriate for people with brain damage. It 'could offer in appropriate cases a structured situation which meets their needs for care and which provides protection for others from their behavioural difficulties' (para. 3.18.5) .

Again, whilst the numbers were small, the proportion of cases in which hospital admission was avoided by the use of other alternative care was considerably higher than it was amongst all those who were referred for assessment. This could suggest a greater reluctance on the part of workers to agree to compulsory detention of people with a mental handicap. None the less, evidence of the alternatives used does not suggest that there are a wider range of resources available to this group. In 8 of the 12 cases in which alternative care was provided, this relied (at least in part) on family care, and in 7 cases it relied on support from social workers. Alternative residential accommodation were used only once and day care twice. Alternative residential care was mentioned in 6 of the 10 cases where people were admitted to hospital in circumstances in which social workers thought this could have been prevented. They were rather more reluctant to suggest that additional family support could have prevented admission, as this was only mentioned in two cases.

The importance of places for people with mental handicap to live away from the parental home is reflected in the Draft Code of Practice's discussion of aftercare needs:

> In the case of mentally handicapped people who are in hospital because of difficulties at their parents' home it is important that the plan for their aftercare in the community should be carefully formulated. Indeed, if the patient is of an age at which he would normally have left his parental home it should be considered whether it might be in his best interests to make other arrangements, even though his parents would like to have him home.
>
> (para. 12.7.8.)

If the intention was that the legislation should only apply in extreme circumstances to people with a mental handicap, difficulties in the parental home should not be a reason for hospital admission. Whilst the numbers are very small, there is still some suggestion that this principle has on occasion been compromised by insufficient resources.

GUARDIANSHIP

This discussion on mental handicap leads naturally to a consideration of guardianship, for it was people with a mental handicap who were most often made the subject of guardianship under the 1959 legislation, although the Percy Commission (1957) had certainly intended it should be a power of relevance to work with all mentally disordered people.

Although intended as an alternative to admission, its use never reached a significant proportion of those compulsorily admitted. By 1978, for example, there were only 138 uses of guardianship and 18,445 compulsory admissions. None the less, extreme variation between local authorities meant that some local authorities were using guardianship with a frequency approaching that of which the Percy Commission might have approved.

The nature and extent of guardianship powers were the subject of much discussion during the debate (reported more fully in Fisher, 1988) that preceded the passing of the 1983 Act and many advocated its substantial extension. The final revision of the powers fell some way short of meeting their hopes. The move away from the paternalistic and all-embracing powers of the 1959 Act formulation and restriction to the three 'essential powers' – to specify place of residence, to require the patient to attend for treatment, and to guarantee access – was largely welcomed. Advocates of the concept of a community treatment order, however, felt that the failure to incorporate the power to consent to treatment seemed likely to restrict the extent to which guardianship would be used more often as a community-based alternative to compulsory admission. This reflected the view expressed in the 1978 review (DHSS, 1978) that it was the failure to take medication that often resulted in those admissions it was hoped the extended use of guardianship might prevent.

Another view of guardianship was to emphasize its potential as a form of protective advocacy for certain groups, particularly people with mental handicap (Gostin, 1983; Durrant, 1983; Gunn, 1986). The principal argument is that guardianship can protect civil rights by establishing formal powers where otherwise 'persuasion' might unreasonably be applied. Examples might be found in the expectations placed on a person with mental handicap to attend a day centre or an old person to enter a part III home without adequate explanation of their right to refuse.

This represents a conceptually different application of guardianship and one that is out of step with legislation concerned principally with the conditions governing compulsory detention in hospital. Hence, for example, the requirement that mental handicap be accompanied by 'abnormal aggression or seriously irresponsible conduct' would seem to exclude the majority of people with mental handicap who might benefit from any protective advocacy. It also appears to us a rather compromised form of advocacy that is not independent of powers to use compulsion.

None the less, there remained in many quarters an expectation that guardianship might be used more often, which was reinforced by the Mental Health Act Commission's Draft Code of Practice. This portrayed guardianship as a clear alternative to admission and, indeed, continued detention of in-patients and asked social services departments to set out clearly their criteria and procedures for taking out guardianship (paras 3.3 to 3.6). Further support for guardianship has come from the view, held particularly by social work practitioners, that the legal obligations entailed can be used as a means of commanding resources that might not otherwise be made available. In particular, guardianship may entail a considerable input of a social worker's time, which is also likely to be under pressure from the demands of statutory child-care work. Hence Dooher suggests:

> A statutory duty placed on the local authority in respect of a particular individual is more likely to attract continued social work involvement and other support services for the individual than a permissive power to provide voluntary support. Thus renewal of guardianship may be sought not because the individual needs continuing restraints but because the order is perceived as guaranteeing Social Services support.
>
> (Dooher, 1989)

Whilst our figures provide some evidence of a substantial increase in the use of guardianship under section 7 of the 1983 Act we are still talking about a relatively infrequently used power. In our study there were 63 such recorded uses of guardianship. Roughly extrapolated this might mean about 200 civil uses of guardianship nationally in the one year period. Such an extrapolation would not reflect continuing territorial variation in consideration of its use however (Table 5.1) and DHSS figures suggest 210 uses equivalent to those we have recorded. Whilst nearly a half of our authorities never actually considered a request for the use of guardianship in the study period, another did so on 27 occasions.

Nor is it clear that guardianship was often seen as an alternative when hospital admission was requested. Guardianship was used only twice in response to requests for detention under sections 2,

3, or 4 and once in response to a request for informal admission. Guardianship did follow an unspecified assessment on 6 occasions and in contrast, of 91 requests for guardianship only 2 resulted in hospital admission. One-half of all uses of guardianship simply followed a request for guardianship to be taken out.

Table 5.1 Variation in the consideration of the use of guardianship

	Number of local authorities
Never	18
Once	8
Twice	5
Three times	4
Four times	3
Five times	1
6–9 times	2
10 + times	1
Total	*42*

One clue to the relatively sparse use of guardianship as an alternative to admission, and confirmation of Anderson-Ford and Halsey's (1984) views that resources would remain a major deterrent to its extended use is provided by this excerpt from one department's policy guidance:

an ASW considering the possibility of guardianship as an alternative to hospital admission should give careful thought to its feasibility with present staffing levels. If there is serious doubt about the ability of an Area Team to allocate the resultant work, which may of course be considerable, an application for guardianship should not be made.

In our study this authority recorded no requests or uses of guardianship nor are there records of its use in the subsequent year.

Table 5.2 The age of people referred for guardianship

Age	<24	25–34	35–44	45–54	55–64	65+
Number	8	14	6	10	9	42
Percentage	9.0	15.7	6.7	11.2	10.1	47.1
S.7 used	6	12	5	7	4	28

The ages of those referred for guardianship are revealing (Table 5.2). Forty-seven per cent of all requests for guardianship concerned over 65s compared with 19 per cent in the study overall. The implication that guardianship was seen as relevant to old people suffering senile dementia is supported by examining the diagnoses of those referred (Figure 5.1). Nearly one-third of those referred for guardianship had a diagnosis of senile dementia (five times the proportion in the study as a whole), whilst mental handicap was the second largest single diagnostic category.

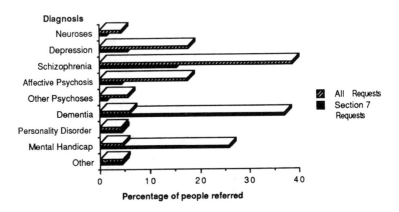

Figure 5.1 Diagnosis of people referred for guardianship

Clearly from our evidence guardianship remains a little used power, with wide local variation in its use, that is selectively applied to certain categories of mentally disordered people. Furthermore, we cannot see it easily becoming a power of wider relevance in the prevention of unnecessary compulsory admission. As we argue in more detail elsewhere (Fisher, 1988), supported by the Draft Code of Practice (Mental Health Act Commission, 1985, para. 3.4), the success of guardianship, rather than nominal compliance with its conditions, depends on the patient's co-operation. If such co-operation can be gained, albeit with an element of persuasion, is an element of compulsion really necessary? Nor can we be persuaded of the merit of guardianship as a means of commanding social services resources. Whilst we accept the difficulty, given the existing priorities within social services departments, of protecting mental health work that does not have the status of a statutory duty, we cannot endorse a situation where the resources to support an individual outside the hospital setting can only be guaranteed by restricting the liberty of someone who, by implication, is prepared to co-operate with that programme of support. In both cases it appears to us that the element of compulsion is made to appear efficacious by deficiencies in existing services and should be unnecessary in good quality community mental health services staffed by skilled workers.

LEGISLATING FOR AFTERCARE

The requirement in section 117 of the 1983 Act that health authorities and social services departments, in co-operation with relevant voluntary agencies, provide aftercare for those subject to detention under section 3 and certain criminal sections has been subject to considerable debate. Local authorities had long been empowered to provide aftercare to ex-psychiatric patients, under the 1968 Health Services and Public Health Act and subsequent legislation, and many hospital social workers in particular had seen the consideration of need for aftercare for *all* discharged patients as good practice.

There was concern, however, about the level of care provided, since echoed by the Audit Commission (1986), and clearly it was felt that special attention should be given through this legislation to ensuring that aftercare for some detained patients was always given serious consideration.

The response to the legislation has been mixed. Only one-third of social services departments in our study reported having specifically established a distinct procedure for section 117. Some reported formal procedures for detailed agreements to be reached and recorded about appropriate aftercare plans for each patient, for key workers to be allocated, and formal reviews carried out. Others simply reported arrangements by the health authority to inform the social services department of each patient detained under the appropriate sections and agreement to invite the appropriate social worker to the ward round where discharge would be discussed.

Some authorities reported that negotiations were still proceeding to establish formal arrangements, but many simply did not see the relevance of the legislation. The reasons for this varied. In one authority it was felt that the formal notification to the social services department of all discharges meant that they could always provide support where necessary and this therefore met the legislation's requirements. In another, multidisciplinary discharge plans were established practice and further direction to provide aftercare thus considered unnecessary. A rather different perspective was provided by one London borough, identified in Chapter 4 as a high-diversion authority. Here, whilst the desirability of providing aftercare was recognized and seen as a long-term goal, it was felt that existing resources would constrain the borough's ability to comply fully with its duties under section 117:

> an unhappy situation which arises inevitably from the passage of legislation without regard to the feasibility of implementation or to the serious damage that would be inflicted on other vulnerable people if it were to be implemented to the letter.

Further evidence of the patchy impact of section 117 is provided by our study figures. Although some of those subject to the 1,728 uses of detention under section 3 recorded in the study year will have remained in hospital voluntarily, or seen the section 3 detention renewed, broadly we might expect to have recorded a similar number of requests for aftercare under section 117. In fact only 291 requests were recorded.

That is not to say necessarily that the majority of those discharged from section 3 were not receiving appropriate aftercare – although a few authorities did openly state that this could sometimes be the case. Nor does it indicate as some critics of our study have suggested, simply a massive under-recording of all requests not directly involving assessment for compulsory detention. Clearly there has in another sense been an under-recording *because* social workers in many authorities simply do not operate within a framework where section 117 has been given local meaning and they do not attach that label to aftercare work that may be carried out with discharged patients. In our view it is clear that whatever the merits of the intentions behind section 117 it does not constitute a consistent legal safeguard to ensure proper aftercare. Good practice is clearly not easily achieved by legislation alone.

THE ROLE OF THE NEAREST RELATIVE

Like the new aftercare duties, the new provisions concerning nearest relatives seem less than perfectly matched to the demands of practice.

Nearest relatives are important people in the eyes of the mental health law and among her or his powers are those connected with the making of an application. The review of the Act had brought about the possibility that this power might be removed, but in the event a conservative lobby, substantially influenced by the National Schizophrenia Fellowship, ensured its survival. Some parts of the country did experience a rise in the number of nearest relative applications immediately after the Act, partly as a result of alleged difficulties in obtaining the services of an ASW to assess for the use of detention. It may also be used where working relationships are strained and the recommending doctor(s) wish to bypass an ASW judgment. None the less it is a rarely used power. In our study there were 95 requests for reports under section 14 following an application for detention by a nearest relative – 59 under section 2 and 36 under section 3. These 95 applications comprise only 1.6 per cent of all applications for detention.

Section 14 itself was intended as a safeguard against nearest relatives who might not be acting in the best interests of the mentally disordered person in applying for his or her compulsory detention. It was originally proposed as a report to be completed by a social worker before detention was applied, but this aspect was lost in the committee stages and therefore its value as a safeguard drastically diluted.

The concern generated within SSDs about the demands of this section – about resources and about quite what the reports should contain – seems a little out of proportion with its apparent use. It is perhaps also worth recording that 37 per cent of these reports were completed by non-ASWs.

The right of nearest relatives to require an ASW assessment (under section 13 (4)) is similarly little used – occurring only on 52 occasions in our study. Only 14 cases of compulsory detention resulted. Although enacted to safeguard the rights of relatives, its use depends almost totally on the ASW's interpretation of her or his statements, thus undermining its relevance. What those involved in securing the enactment of section 13 (4) clearly did not realize is that, during almost every case of potential compulsory admission where the nearest relative is present, a statement will be made like 'Something's got to be done', which could be interpreted as a request under section 13 (4). Its relevance during an assessment is thus extremely limited. Furthermore, few social services departments would advocate a policy of widespread publicity for such a power.

MENTAL HEALTH REVIEW TRIBUNALS AND OPINIONS RE: TREATMENT

It is perhaps surprising, given the emphasis in section 13 on the approved social worker's role in determining whether hospital is the right setting for treatment when detention commences, that the 1983 Rules governing Mental Health Review Tribunals (MHRTs) make no reference to social workers, whether approved or not. They are neither required to submit reports nor to give evidence in tribunal hearings.

None the less, we would have expected their fairly frequent involvement. On rare occasions the social services department will be required to submit reports to tribunals on people detained under guardianship. But more significantly one of the reports hospitals must submit to tribunals for detained patients is an up-to-date social circumstances report, which will be important in determining the feasibility of discharge. This will usually be provided by hospital social workers.

Because there had been some concern within social services departments about the burden this might create, given the projected increase in Mental Health Review Tribunals, these reports were included in the SSRG monitoring exercise. Only 352 such reports following a section 2 or 3 detention were recorded plus 75 for tribunals following a section 37 detention. This would indicate reports nationally to about 1,300 tribunals. This is certainly an underestimate but clues as to why this has occurred may indicate interesting differences in attitudes to these reports.

The major focus of our research was on approved social workers' assessments of the need for detention and we have established that, in several study authorities, staff not called upon to make these assessments were only peripherally involved in the research, if at all. This effectively excluded a large number of hospital social workers, who provide the majority of reports to MHRTs, although many hospital social workers, including those who were approved, did participate.

One-third of the reports recorded in our study were provided by ASWs working outside a hospital setting. They also reported other instances of involvement with tribunals – providing evidence orally and/or helping clients to prepare for tribunals. In contrast, hospital workers rarely recorded other instances of helping. They also recorded the provision of information for hospital managers in a variety of other circumstances and further enquiries have shown that, on occasions, this information will subsequently have been used as reports to MHRTs. This may have contributed to the under-recording of MHRT reports but may also in itself be indicative of a different attitude to such work. Although there will undoubtedly be exceptions, the community based ASW may be more geared up to a quasi-independent assessment role in general and be more likely to see these reports as significant bits of work under the Act and record them as such. The hospital based workers in contrast may have been providing such reports for years and see them as much more part of their routine duty in providing a social-work service within the hospital setting. Whether this makes any difference to the value of the evidence provided in those reports is something that may merit further consideration.

In contrast to the prominence given in the pre-reform debate to the regulations concerning consent to treatment, the introduction of the second opinion procedure received scant attention amongst those concerned with the social worker's altered role. It is not mentioned in the detailed procedural guidance provided by some of our study authorities to ASWs and the uncertainty of social workers called on to provide consultative advice to second opinion doctors is well established (for example, see Williams, 1988).

Only 169 cases of such advice being provided by social workers were recorded in our study. Even given that psychologists and other therapists can be called upon to provide this advice, this also seems a low figure – particularly given the extent of recourse to the second opinion procedure reported in one region by Williams. Indeed, a rough extrapolation based on the figures in the Second Biennial Report of the Mental Health Act Commission (1987) would suggest for our study area a figure of over 500. Again, however, our central focus on approved social worker assessments may have influenced the recording of these incidents. The 38 (26 per cent) incidents recorded by approved social workers outside hospital may well represent fairly their involvement in those formal consultations about treatment, but many consultations with hospital social workers will not be included. This can once more be partly explained by the effective exclusion of some hospital social workers from the project but also probably, as was explicitly confirmed by workers in one or two authorities, by their perception of such advice as nothing exceptional but part of their routine hospital social work task.

Quite how independent the social worker's view can be in such circumstances was touched upon in the pre-reform discussion though hardly resolved by the absence of any real guidance as to whether hospital social workers should be seen as being suitably detached for approved social worker status. The regulations governing Mental Health Review Tribunals and consultations about second opinions do not specify that approved social workers need be involved and our evidence suggests that they rarely are. If the exercising of an independent professional judgment representing the social perspective on mental illness is desirable, and if approved social worker status enhances the ability to provide that independence – a basic tenet of the Act – then current circumstances do not meet that ideal.

SECTION 136

Section 136 of the 1983 Mental Health Act allows the police to remove from a public place someone who appears to be mentally disordered and in need of immediate care and control and hold them for up to 72 hours in order that they be assessed by a doctor and an approved social worker. It had been largely untouched by the process of reform preceding the 1983 Act. Although there had been recommendations by BASW and MIND for a 24-hour power based on criteria of arrestibility and dangerousness, these were dismissed by the 1976 White Paper and most of the subsequent discussions revolved around the unsuitability of police stations rather than hospitals as places of safety and on emphasizing that the power lapses after the two examinations. Neither was BASW's request that it be made a requirement that social services departments be notified of the use of section 136 heeded or much thought given to the apparent contradiction between the new training proposed for ASWs and the implication that any police officer is sufficiently skilled to be able to detect probable mental disorder.

This probably reflected the infrequency with which section 136 appeared to be used. Whilst strictly speaking it is not a form of compulsory admission it was recorded as the section governing 6.8 per cent of compulsory admissions in 1976 and although this had risen to 10.7 per cent by 1982, this did not appear to impact upon the reform process. The figures rose again to 12.4 per cent in 1984 before declining subsequently.

These figures, however, both appear to underestimate the use of section 136 nationally and do not do justice to the extreme local variations in its use. One problem in considering the use of section 136 is that there is no universal procedure for its recording. Some police forces use a form when detention occurs in a police station, others when they remove someone to a hospital, and at other times there seems to be nothing recorded at all. In consequence, although we know the DHSS figures on admissions to hospital provide only a partial measure of the use of section 136, there is no way of knowing what proportion these are of the total.

Although there remains a degree of controversy about whether absence of an ASW assessment is unlawful (Mental Health Act Commission, 1987; Rogers and Faulkner, 1987) it is none the less clear that, contrary to the *spirit* of the legislation, social workers are rarely involved in assessments under section 136. Rogers and Faulkner report social workers' assessments in only 8.6 per cent of the uses of section136 that they studied and our study records only 126 such social worker assessments when DHSS figures might suggest 600 admissions as likely in our study areas. In fact, social workers in our study had a greater involvement in assessments following the use of section 136 than this indicates. There were, for example, 510 occasions when police requests for 'unspecified assessments' were made. We suspect that a number of these may have followed situations where the police considered that they were acting under section 136 but where, in the absence of clear documentation, this was not clear to the social worker and so they recorded the incident as an unspecified assessment. Furthermore, inspection of the monitoring forms has shown a large number of occasions when police have taken individuals to psychiatric hospitals – presumably largely under section 136 – and social workers have subsequently been called in by the psychiatric services, often towards the end of the 72 hour period, to assess for a section 2 application or to complete an unspecified assessment. Because of the nature of the request, these have also not been recorded as section 136 assessments. The difficulty of assessing accurately the total number of such requests included in our research reflects, therefore, the ambiguous status of section 136 detentions.

The majority of requests we have unambiguously recorded were to assess someone held in a police station. This parallels the findings of Rogers and Faulkner's (1987) study in which all but one person so detained were seen by a social worker.

The most common practice, therefore, appears to be that where someone is detained under section 136 in a police station, the social worker is called in to assess frequently, but within hospitals it is left to the psychiatric services to call in a social worker if and when it is considered appropriate. In a number of cases this clearly means that section 136 is *de facto* being used as a means of detaining for assessment for up to 72 hours without a social worker's assessment, a practice also identified and criticized within the Second Biennial Report of the Mental Health Act Commission (1987:32).

This is not a generally applicable pattern however. We asked our study authorities about specific agreements reached with the local police over section 136 and nearly a half reported that no such agreements had been made. Several reported automatic notification by the police to social services departments when section 136 was used including two authorities where the usual place of safety was a hospital. Others refer only to an 'expectation' that they would be called in and two that the formal arrangement was for a psychiatrist to be called to make an assessment at the police station (and presumably decide whether an ASW decision was needed). In one authority the agreement was of a rather different nature. The police took individuals to the hospital (the usual place of safety) where they regarded responsibility to decide whether 'the medical examination and interview *permitted* [our italics] under section 136' were appropriate to transfer to the health authority .

Several authorities reported that admissions under section 136 should not occur or at least would not be normal practice but clearly this is still a regular practice in some authorities as the DHSS figures reveal. These may diminish as more local authorities develop formal arrangements with the police. Two authorities specifically cited adverse criticism of the use of the section for admission as reasons for recent or current renegotiation of those arrangements.

One element of criticism of the use of section 136 has been that it has been used disproportionately often to detain black people (Hitch and Clegg, 1980, Rogers and Faulkner, 1987). Our figures, as we have said, only cover one part of all such referrals, but certainly 16 per cent of those requests involve non-white people (10 per cent Afro-Caribbeans) compared with an estimated 6.4 per cent (based on census figures and probably an underestimate) in the study population and 12 per cent of all requests.

They show a similar over-representation of men – 61.5 per cent of requests for 136 concerned men as opposed to 43.5 per cent of all requests – and there was a concentration in particular age bands – 66 per cent of these requests involving those aged 25–44 compared with 39.4 per cent of all requests. Section 136 assessments were distributed unevenly – 48 per cent were recorded in just four of our study authorities. Given the imbalance in DHSS figures on admissions, it is hardly surprising that 41 per cent came from London boroughs (which covered only 15 per cent of the population of our study areas) whilst only 10 per cent came from the metropolitan districts (which covered 28 per cent). Even within London there was an imbalance with 37 per cent of cases occurring in one authority.

This should not be seen as a full indication of the distribution of the use of section 136, however. This does vary greatly, with 88.7 per cent of all admissions recorded under the section occurring in the combined Thames regions in 1985 (DHSS, 1986), but as we have suggested our figures record those occurrences where assessments by ASWs took place and, by and large, therefore probably *exclude* those recorded as admissions in DHSS figures. Only 18.4 per cent of these assessments resulted in a formal admission and 33.6 per cent in informal admissions.

Overall, it is clear to us that ASWs are not in all areas being drawn automatically into assessments following the use of section

136 as surely the spirit of the Act as a whole would intend. If such assessments are to occur routinely, formal agreements between police forces, health authorities, and social services departments of the kind already achieved in many areas need to be reached. Ideally these should include direct notification to the social services department by the police of the use of section 136 and this may, as Rogers and Faulkner (1987) suggest, require the police to document more clearly when this power is being used.

THE ORGANIZATIONAL RESPONSE TO THE MENTAL HEALTH ACT

We highlighted in Chapter 3 the hopeful expectation by many observers that the 1983 Act marked a greater recognition of the potential contribution of the social perspective on mental disorder to be embodied in an extended role for its major proponent in practice – the social worker. In consequence a radical reappraisal of the work of social services departments was anticipated – examining the need for new resources, the location of mental health social work within the organization, and the structures guiding and supporting the social workers providing it.

We had hoped at one point in the research to classify authorities for comparative purposes on the basis of their approach to mental health work and the challenge of the 1983 Act, but reality proved to be too untidy to achieve a consistent and meaningful categorization. Authorities with extensive commitments to training in mental health social work were not necessarily those with most commitment to developing alternative resources in the community or to protecting staff time to work with mentally disordered people. Nor were they necessarily those with specialist advisory and support staff. This lack of coincidence between indicators of the kind and level of service provided was further complicated by the different starting points of authorities before 1983. A positive response to the Act may have indicated a positive attitude to mental health social work or perhaps simply a low baseline of provision and/or awareness.

We asked the authorities in the study about the specific organizational and resource changes prompted by the Act. Twelve (of 36 providing this detailed information) reported none at all. Fifteen reported additional expenditure on training, though the scale of response varied from the appointment of additional staff to an extra £1500 in the annual training budget. Three authorities appointed specialist advisors on mental disorder and two set up special teams to deal with mental health social work, but of course several already had such arrangements. Twelve reported the appointment of extra social work staff, ranging in scale from one part-timer in a London borough to six workers in one county. Another county authority implemented a large-scale joint-financed scheme to deal with developments in mental health work but identified other major influences on its formulation. Half a dozen reported new physical resources – drop-in centres, day centres, and hostels – which they saw as direct responses to the Act. Of course all of these developments will have also had other influences behind them and often the Act was simply the final justification for implementing ideas that had been present for some time. Only five authorities actually reported comprehensive assessments and development plans that reflected anything approaching a wholesale endorsement of the idea of an extended role for their department in mental health services, and these were far from consistent in their approach to some of the major issues in formulating such a comprehensive programme.

Decisions about the numbers and location of approved social workers were one such issue. The creation of this specifically designated social worker, who, it was originally intended, should not only have to undertake special training but also should sit and pass an examination, gave new impetus to the unresolved debate about the merits of specialism and genericism that had lingered since Seebohm. Was mental health work better seen as a specialism within social work and thus only undertaken by those workers who had undergone ASW training, or should all social workers be enabled to do mental health work as required? Should those workers who were approved under the terms of the Act be brought together in specialist teams, should they be a part of short term or intake teams, or should they be members of long term generic teams? And what about hospital social workers? Should those working in psychiatric hospitals or wards be regarded as *de facto* experts in mental health work, or should their independence from the doctors with whom they work be viewed with suspicion and disqualify them from the possibility of becoming approved?

These questions provoked many different answers. Hey (1985)

quotes a meeting of twenty-four social services directors, all from London boroughs, at which estimates of the numbers of ASWs needed ranged from 6 to 100. Decisions left individual ASWs in some departments unhappy about what they saw to be the implications for their ability to fulfill the role of the ASW. For example, in one authority in our study, some ASWs located in intake teams were concerned that it would be difficult for them to maintain continuing involvement with clients following assessment. Decisions relating to the appropriate number of ASWs produced conflicting concerns: in authorities where it was decided that comparatively small numbers of social workers should be approved, there was concern that the service would be stretched too thinly and social workers would be called on to assess people whom they did not know; in authorities where the decision was that all (or as many as possible) social workers should be approved, there was concern that individual experience would be so thinly spread that it would not be possible to build up confidence or expertise.

Our evidence confirms the very different conclusions authorities had reached about what was a 'sufficient number of approved social workers' (section 114).The number of social workers recording assessments ranged from 14 in two of the authorities to 139 in another. Admittedly the latter was a county authority whilst the other two were comparatively small metropolitan districts, but a county covering a much larger geographical area returned forms from 91 social workers. There does not appear to be any close association between the size of the authority and the number of social workers involved.

The number of workers per 100,000 adult population ranged from 0.65 in one metropolitan authority to 5.5 in one London borough. In terms of type of authority, shire counties showed the least variation in rates – from a low of 0.95 in one county to a high of 1.97 in another. Hey's (1985) observation of the variation of opinion about the numbers of ASWs required in London is confirmed by our findings: whilst three London boroughs had the highest rate per 100,000 population at 5.5, 4.06, and 3.0 respectively, three London boroughs had less than one worker per 100,000 adult population.

ASSESSMENT – A RARE EVENT FOR THE WORKER

One very basic indicator of the extent to which ASWs can build up their skills and experience in undertaking assessments is the number they are called on to undertake. In 35 of the social services departments we looked at, the most common number of ASW assessments undertaken was 1. Of the 1,762 social workers involved, 525 of them (30 per cent) recorded only one assessment during the year in which the monitoring took place. This in itself must heighten concern about their ability to provide an assessment based on both an understanding of mental disorder and how this can be expressed by individuals in very different circumstances and with very different characteristics, and on a knowledge of available resources that might be a source of 'care and treatment'. In an unfamiliar situation there is a danger that concern about the form an assessment should take might take precedence over its content. In this particular context where the expertise of the psychiatrist is more publicly recognized than is that of the ASW, there is the added danger of deference to the acknowledged 'expert' and the avoidance of risk.

There were considerable differences between authorities both in the numbers of assessments undertaken by different workers and in the distribution of assessments between workers. At the extremes, the maximum number of assessments undertaken by any one worker was 7 in one authority and 42 in another. There were some authorities in which there was a comparatively equitable distribution of assessments so that no workers stood out as having a particularly unusual pattern of work, whilst in one authority one worker did 41 of the 149 assessments recorded during the year, almost twice as many as the worker recording the next highest number. This pattern reoccurs in slightly less extreme form in four other authorities. Of these five authorities, two were London boroughs, two were metropolitan districts, and one was a large shire county; again geographical explanations seem out of place. If we look at the average number of assessments undertaken by each worker, this ranged from 2.3 in one authority to 13.9 in another. Both were metropolitan districts. In the first there were a total of 77 assessments undertaken by 34 workers, in the second 236 assessments were undertaken by 17 workers. This confirms that decisions about appropriate numbers of ASWs have not been determined by workloads alone.

Over all, just as we suggested in Chapter 4 that we could find no consistent organizational pattern associated with high or low levels of diversion or detention, nor could the variation in the numbers and distribution of assessments be consistently explained. In two of the authorities where a *de facto* specialization – with one worker doing far more assessments than any others – was recorded, this appeared a deliberate policy. In one authority, finance had been provided specifically for an ASW to do 'admission' work, whilst in the other, one hospital ASW dealt with all referrals under the Act for two area teams. Yet the authority with the most extreme example of this pattern of work reported having no specifically designated specialist mental health workers.

Similarly those authorities in which there was a comparatively small range in the number of assessments undertaken by different social workers described very different patterns of organization and responses to the issue of whether ASWs should be seen as specialists or not. Some had community mental health teams in which ASWs were based, one had a crisis intervention team, others had mental health specialists based in area teams or hospitals, and still others had large numbers of ASWs, none of whom were described as specialist mental health workers.

Another element of variation between authorities was the extent to which they had been concerned to set up their own internal systems to monitor the work arising from the Act, which again seemed unrelated to organizational structure.

These results are indicative of a continuing confusion over the appropriate organizational pattern for the provision of mental health services, confusion over how to most effectively deploy and support the scarce resource of the approved social worker. As such they may be seen as reinforcement of the concern of many supporters of the potential of the 1983 Act – that developments in managerial and supervisory systems might not be sufficient to provide the right environment for the ASWs to practise their enhanced skills.

We are not arguing here that one set organizational pattern is right. There are different patterns of work that appear to contain elements of good practice as we describe in Appendix 4. None the less, some consistency in the principles apparently underlying the deployment of ASWs would give us more confidence that there was some shared understanding of the appropriate content and organization of mental health practice.

What, though, of the impact of these different organizational choices? Whilst our project was not designed to evaluate different structures for ASWs, we have been able to gain some idea of their influence on some key issues.

OUTCOMES ACCORDING TO THE NUMBERS AND LOCATION OF ASWS

Our previous discussion has pointed out the difficulty of reaching firm conclusions about why outcomes of assessments are rather different in some areas compared with others. The number of ASWs is another potentially relevant factor in this complex picture, but adding in this piece of the jigsaw still makes it difficult to draw straightforward conclusions. The high diversion authorities we identified in Appendix 4, authorities A and B, had 0.69 and 1.5 workers per 100,000 adult population; the 'average' authorities, C and D, had rates of 1.1, and 1.9, whilst the low diversion authorities, E and F, had worker rates of 1.72 and 4.06. Whilst one can highlight authorities A and F as apparently indicating that concentrating work in a few workers can lead to high diversion rates, there is no similar association between worker rates and outcomes in the other highlighted authorities.

Our results none the less challenge some of the easy assumptions that might be made about the ASW location most conducive to avoidance of compulsory detention. The lowest level of *compulsion* following assessment for sections 2 and 3 resulted from assessments carried out by emergency duty team social workers (EDTs), and in the case of referrals for section 2 assessments, EDT social workers were also able to prevent the need for *any* hospital admission more often than workers in any other location. They were second to intake team workers in finding alternative care following section 3 requests.

Difference in outcomes of section 4 assessments showed far less variation according to worker location, although once again EDT workers were more often able to find alternative care to prevent admission. The only circumstance in which EDT workers were less successful, having the highest compulsory admission rate and the

115

lowest rate of prevention, was when they undertook 'not specified' assessments.

A common assumption is that social workers working out of normal office hours, with limited access to information, advice from colleagues, and access to resources will be less able to prevent admission to hospital. Expressed in terms of the civil rights of those being assessed, the question is asked whether their needs for care and treatment can be assessed appropriately when access to sources of such care and treatment may be restricted. Yet our results suggest that this assumption is far from being supported in practice. Why should this be so? One suggestion could be that, almost by definition, EDT workers are more used to responding to what are perceived to be crises than those who work during normal office hours. When every incident is a 'crisis' , there may be a heightening of discrimination between those circumstances in which danger is real, and those in which behaviour is disturbing but not actually constituting a danger. Working in a high degree of isolation, EDT workers may also need to develop particular skills in drawing on whatever resources are available to them to respond to the needs of people referred. The apparent contradiction in the outcomes of the 'not specified' requests can be explained by the greater likelihood of those requests being appropriate requests under the Act during periods covered by emergency duty. When access to professionals is more difficult, a higher motivation based on a higher degree of certainty about the problem may well be expected.

If the previous suggestion is at least a partial explanation for the observed differences, it has implications for the organization and management of ASWs during office hours. It tends to support the arguments of those who claim that only by having considerable experience of undertaking assessments can ASWs build up the necessary skills and knowledge to act as an effective, independent assessor able to challenge, where necessary, the medical view.

Both the number and proportion of incidents referred to EDT workers varied considerably between authorities, adding to the very different patterns of work on which our overall results draw. Overall, approximately one-quarter of all incidents were recorded by EDT workers, but this varied between less than 4 per cent in one London borough, to almost 50 per cent in one Midlands authority. This cannot be explained by differences in the nature of the emergency duty service provided by authorities as few differences in the time during which the service operated or in any other aspects of the service were reported to us. One possible explanation is that in areas where mental health work is seen as a low priority or is simply unpopular, workers may delay responding to such referrals until the time at which they become the responsibility of the emergency duty service. This type of behaviour would be likely to contribute to an increasing specialism in mental health work amongst EDT workers, and its continuing low-priority, 'dirty work' designation by area team workers.

Where our results do reinforce both the fears and assumptions of some commentators is in relation to the outcomes of assessments carried out by ASWs based in hospitals. The percentage of compulsory detentions following section 2 and 3 assessments by hospital workers was higher than following assessments by workers in any of the other locations we looked at, and the use of alternative care was lower – falling to less than 2 per cent of outcomes of section 3 assessments. Nor is this simply a consequence of the fact that many of those assessed by hospital based ASWs were already in hospital at the time of assessment (see chapter 4) because hospital social workers more often agreed to compulsion being applied for those *both* in and out of hospital. This reinforces the concern at how apparently equal rights under the legislation can be compromised by the circumstances in which those rights are exercised. It also suggests that ASWs working in hospital teams have particular needs both for training and support in carrying out their duties in very different circumstances from their community based colleagues.

The extent to which hospital social workers were seen to play a central role in assessments arising from the legislation varied considerably from authority to authority. Overall, their involvement was greater than that of emergency duty workers – just over one-third of incidents were recorded by hospital social workers, but the variation between authorities was also greater. Less than 1 per cent of incidents were dealt with by hospital workers in two metropolitan districts, compared with 59 per cent in one London borough. Two other authorities should be mentioned here that were singled out in Chapter 4 as being amongst those with the highest levels of diversion. One had only 3 per cent of incidents dealt with by hospital social workers, which falls in line with the implication in our discussion on p.117 that there may well be a firm link between higher rates of diversion and large numbers of assessments falling to ASWs working outside hospitals. The other, in contrast, had the highest proportion of incidents dealt with by hospital-based workers: 93 per cent. However, this was the authority with a crisis intervention team very different from most hospital social work teams and with the most clearly articulated policy of avoiding detention. This example thus serves to reinforce our more general view that whilst organizational structures may not be unimportant, it is rather clearly thought out and consistently supported policy choices that most clearly influence the pattern of use of compulsory detention.

Being based in an intake team as opposed to a long term community team did not appear to make it more difficult for ASWs to avoid the use of compulsion or find alternative care to prevent hospital admission. In fact compulsory admission was the outcome of a slightly higher percentage of assessments by long term team workers. It was unusual for approved social workers to be based in intake teams. Overall, less than 10 per cent of incidents were dealt with by intake teams with two London boroughs standing out as the exceptions to this picture with 35 per cent and 41 per cent of incidents recorded by intake workers.

However, good practice in mental health work cannot be indicated solely by reference to the immediate outcome of the assessment. We have already highlighted the tendency within mental health social work to make one-off responses to crises rather than provide the continuing support that may prevent crises from occurring. We explored, therefore, the potential effect of different locations on the continuity of contact social workers might have with those they were called upon to assess.

As one might expect, intake team social workers assessed people who were on active caseloads less frequently than other workers (Table 5.3) and those previously known, but not currently on an active caseload, more often. This suggests little continuity of contact with those they were assessing, particularly as those already known to the department may have been on another worker's caseload or in receipt of some quite different service. Yet intake workers had the lowest proportion of incidents concerning someone entirely unknown to the department, calling into question the distinction made between long term workers assessing their own clients and intake workers being called upon to assess new clients.

Table 5.3 Referral status of people assessed according to worker location

	Person unknown	*On active caseload*	*'Closed case'*
Intake workers	37.8	23.6	38.6
EDT workers	53.7	24.5	21.8
Hospital workers	46.8	32.3	20.9
Long term workers	48.2	28.3	23.5

The deployment of ASWs in intake teams may then be less problematic to continuity of service than some have argued although the figures for continuing involvement following assessment (Table 5.4) show they were less often able personally to retain involvement than long term workers. Emergency duty workers were those least likely and hospital workers the most likely to retain cases. Clearly, because of their location, continuing involvement following assessment is one of the advantages of having hospital social workers as ASWs. None the less, this would be outweighed in many eyes by the greater propensity they show to agree to admission that makes that continuing involvement more likely. Overall, whatever the location of the workers concerned, the prospects of continuity of involvement seem small, although as we have suggested in several parts of our analysis, the picture was very different in individual authorities with, for example, the proportion of previously known and unknown clients referred to intake workers ranging from 0 to 100 per cent and of hospital workers retaining personal involvement ranging from 0 to 95 per cent.

Table 5.4 Involvement following assessment according to worker location

	Personal involvement continued	*Referred to another worker*	*Case closed*
Intake workers	30.9	35.9	33.1
EDT workers	8.7	71.2	20.1
Hospital workers	47.1	31.0	21.9
Longterm workers	41.7	33.7	24.5

THE PROSPECTS FOR A SOCIAL RESPONSE TO MENTAL DISORDER

The analysis presented in Chapter 4 suggested that, despite resource limitations and evidence of extreme differences between areas, ASWs in some authorities have achieved modest success in shaping the use of the different sections of the 1983 Mental Health Act and in putting into effect the principle of the least restrictive alternative. Any hope that this signalled a widespread and consistent recognition of the validity of the contribution of the social perspective to understanding the origin of mental disorder and forming appropriate strategies for managing the distress resulting from it has been exposed as an illusion by the analysis of this chapter. Apart from the rather important paucity of any consideration of the role of the social worker in work with voluntary patients, other key areas of the 1983 legislation consistently fall short of reinforcing that position.

Section 136, for example, although only a repeat of the same section under the 1959 Act, is clearly supposed to establish the need for an approved social worker assessment. Admissions initially based on the intervention of the police and then assessment of medical practitioners alone are not intended to occur. Yet *de facto* admissions, avoiding the balancing opinion and quasi-legal safeguard of the ASW's assessment appear to be common.

Similarly admissions on the application of the nearest relative contradict the principle of that safeguard. A social circumstances report is required but *after* admission, and it does not have to be provided by a social worker who is approved. Despite arguments about the restricted availability of social workers in rural areas, it is difficult not to attribute some credibility to the notion that it was the fear of strike action by social workers if they *had* to be involved in every compulsory admission that led to this procedure being retained.

Such inconsistencies in the commitment to the involvement of ASWs in decisions to initially detain people are compounded by their views not being required in critical decisions reviewing the continuing validity of detention and in decisions about appropriate treatment. The weakness of the legislation concerning aftercare is another clear signal that there is no consistent conception of the role of the ASW throughout the process of care and treatment.

To some extent, of course, social work has not rushed to embrace these tasks wholeheartedly. The Association of Directors of Social Services, mindful of the difficulties of taking on new duties whilst uncertain of the resource implications, were rather less enthusiastic than BASW about producing an extensive list of work that had to be handled by approved social workers. Nor does the apparent lack of agreement about whether ASWs should be specialists or genericists, where they should be located, and whether they should be thus encouraged to retain a continuity of involvement with mentally disordered clients suggest a clear and widely recognized idea of the role of the social worker in the management of mental disorder.

The Mental Health Act Commission seems mindful of some of the inconsistencies we have highlighted and is trying to move forward within the limits of the existing legislation. For example, they are pressing for multidisciplinary aftercare plans to be formally drawn up and reviewed in all local authorities (Mental Health Act Commission, 1987:66). Whether their work or further alterations to the legislative framework are likely to take forward commitment to the social perspective is doubtful. Of course, legislative change may be necessary to permit more involvement of social workers in key decisions concerning care plans but on its own this is unlikely to succeed. In our view what is urgently required is a new framework for mental health social work that spells out clearly the potential contribution of the social worker and allied personnel *throughout* the process of care and treatment of mentally disordered people. We would have expected such a framework to have underpinned the content of ASW training and it is with a consideration of that training, in the light of our results, that we conclude this chapter.

THE CONTEXT OF ASW TRAINING

During our research, ASW training was influenced by conflicting pressures: to produce sufficient ASWs to meet demand for work and yet to provide a sufficient test of their competence to counter public disquiet about standards of social work training. Responsibility for the latter fell to CCETSW, which had no experience of setting national examinations and had played no significant part in developing the role of the ASW in the legislation. Its background did not therefore inspire mental health practitioners with confidence.

The examination system soon ran into trouble. First CCETSW set a quota of 2,500 on the number of examination places (CCETSW, 1987b), which conflicted with local authorities estimates of needing 6,500 ASWs. Union resistance to non-negotiated postqualification assessment of their members followed and the result was the development of a dual system of 'full' approval for up to 5 years for those who had passed the examination and 'transitional' approval for up to 2 years for those who had received appropriate training but had not been examined. Compared with demand for 6,500 ASWs, the examination system had by late 1985 passed 1,663 (CCETSW, 1987b). At a later stage the inevitable bottleneck led to the extension of transitional approval, which became the principal method of ensuring sufficient numbers of ASWs. By far the majority of ASWs in our study were thus 'transitionally' approved.

Behind this lay several important issues in mental health social work. The inexperience of its principal training body in mental health social work and in setting standards for professional practice exposed how unprepared social work was for an extension of its role. CCETSW's emphasis on medical and legal knowledge produced an uneven training agenda where the learning of technical aspects became overvalued at the expense of the development of social work practice skills (which were not tested in the examination). The hidden agenda of specialization, promoted by many psychiatrists who envisaged the reintroduction of the mental health specialist of the pre-Seebohm years and fuelled by many within social work who sought an alliance with the prestigious profession of psychiatry, led to confusion about the direction of training: was it to produce social workers who knew about mental health or mental health professionals who knew about social work? DHSS pressure to restrict the number of ASWs also came into conflict with SSD pressure to expand their number, either for simple reasons concerned with the planning of duty rotas to provide cover, or for more complex reasons connected with the desire to promote the mental health component of social work at a non-specialist level.

The DHSS supported its arguments by reference to the relatively small number of compulsory admissions, failing to see either that ASWs were needed to meet demands for assessments of which only two-thirds resulted in compulsory admission (Fisher *et al.*, 1984) or that the ASW might have a significant role to play in more than just these assessments. Perhaps most ominously, ASW training was minimally funded: it was not unusual for an authority to be told that an extra £10,000 had been included in the Rate Support Grant without negotiation as to whether this in any way matched the real costs, and, if it was a rate-capped authority, it was of course highly unlikely that ASW training would be seen as such a high priority as to warrant the earmarking of this money. In common with a growing trend in social welfare legislation in the early 1980s, much was promised in the Act but resources to make its goals achievable were lacking.

IMPLICATIONS FOR TRAINING

Given this context for ASW training, what are the particular lessons from the research?

- Action under the Act is a relatively rare event, even for ASWs. The annual mean number of assessments per ASW was 4.3. Moreover, some aspects of the Act (such as section 136 assessments or assessment of people with mental handicap) are extremely rare. There is thus a genuine tension between appointing a sufficient number of ASWs to provide cover and ensuring that each ASW has a chance to exercise her or his skills. Given the relatively small size of the population at risk of detention, many authorities have resolved this dilemma in favour of providing cover: the question is whether a parallel training strategy has been developed to prepare ASWs to use a set of skills and knowledge so rarely.
- We have shown that the use of the Act varies considerably around the country. Exploration of the reasons for such variation, whether it is appropriate and, where necessary, how such variation might be challenged in practice ought to receive attention in training.
- We have also shown that it is possible to identify at least some characteristics of the population at risk of detention under

the Act. For example: nearly 20 per cent of those referred were aged 65-plus; there is a particular issue about work with married women with young children and with young Black men (see Chapter 6) ; unemployment was a characteristic of the circumstances of 72 per cent of men and 54 per cent of women of employable age. Although these factors will vary greatly between SSDs, it should now be possible to design training in recognition of the characteristics of people most likely to be referred.

- Despite modest overall levels of diversion, in many areas we found a substantial level of difference between the recommendations of doctors and the outcome as influenced by the ASW. It is often assumed that the operation of the Act involves a consensus of professional judgments about the right course of action. A contrary view is that an interplay of different professional perspectives, sometimes involving a degree of conflict, is the best safeguard for the prospective patient. Clearly, if the latter view forms part of social work's approach to the role of the ASW, and given the incidence of disagreement between recommending doctors and ASWs, some recognition in terms of training for the management of interprofessional conflict is required.

- The emphasis on alternatives to detention is none the less difficult to achieve in practice, partly because of the lack of resources but also partly because of the tendency to conceptualize alternatives as accommodation rather than a package of care co-ordinated by the ASW. ASW training should therefore focus on the typical circumstances of referral and on the skills involved in designing alternative care packages.

- The evidence is that ASWs frequently persuade those subject to recommendations for detention to enter or stay in hospital informally: over 13 per cent of those subject to recommendations under sections 2, 3, or 4 ended up in hospital as informal patients. Such persuasion can be to the patient's benefit, in the sense that hospital treatment is thought necessary and best achieved without the stigma of compulsion. On the other hand there is the danger that patients are threatened with the use of compulsion and comply only because of this threat. Clearly, the handling of such situations in such a way as to give prospective patients the choice of informality without threatening them is a skilled task for which a training focus would be relevant.

• The use of detention is just a small event in the lives of people whose needs for service from mental health services are extensive. Yet 24 per cent of referrals were closed after initial contact. Often this may be rationalized as a legitimate response given that 85 per cent of those referred under sections 2, 3, or 4 were admitted (either formally or informally) to hospital and are seen as in some sense 'safe'. If such people are to be given more than a fleeting service, there are clear implications for SSD policy and resources: it is also likely that the attitudes of ASWs will need some attention during their training to orient them towards integrating their ASW task into a full social work service.

Overall, therefore, the research points to the need for training to be better focused on the most likely types of referrals and most likely types of clients; on exploring skills in persuasion without coercion and in interprofessional conflict; on challenging ASWs to design packages of alternative care rather than merely performing an assessment of the need for detention; and developing their commitment to and understanding of a role that continues throughout the care and treatment of mentally disordered people.

The current training requirements for ASWs involve completing a 60-day course that has itself been approved by CCETSW (CCETSW 1987a). Despite more emphasis on practice skills, the curriculum prescribed remains unevenly weighted towards a knowledge component that reflects the concerns of the original examination. There is also an emphasis on 'clinical knowledge' (para. 2.3) that appears to reinforce the primacy of psychiatric language in understanding the lives and circumstances of people referred for action under the mental health legislation. In contrast there is no reference in the core curriculum to intervention methods within mental health social work that are based on specifically social or psychological perspectives, such as developments in behavioural social work (Hudson, 1982) or in working with support networks (Taylor and Huxley, 1984). There is inherent in this the danger of reinforcing the view that mental health social work is devoid of its own intervention technology and

125

that the role of the ASW consists principally of the application of legal and clinical knowledge.

However, in embarking on discussions about refresher training for practising ASWs, CCETSW have drawn on findings from this project both about 'the social structural environment for mental health work and implications for training therefrom' (Wright, 1988 : 3), and in suggesting that training may need to include the development of agency mental health strategies. CCETSW London and South Eastern Region have also provided funding for a training package, based on our findings, that specifically focuses on the social circumstances, rather than the clinical diagnosis of people referred as the starting point for assessment (Newton, 1988). It is too early to say whether this will lead to radical shifts in basic ASW training which will provide them with their own language of assessment and enable them to develop particular social work skills based on social rather than psychiatric understandings. But it does represent some movement in the right direction.

Chapter 6

THE SOCIAL PERSPECTIVE ON MENTAL DISORDER AND MENTAL HEALTH PRACTICE

Our argument throughout this book has been that the medical perspective on mental health and mental disorder needs to be balanced by a social perspective. Although this is *implied* by giving social services departments statutory responsibilities under the mental health legislation, the dominance of the medical perspective over definitions of mental disorder and how it should be treated, and over resources currently available to help those with mental health problems, is such that the social perspective has not really had the chance to show what it can offer.

In this chapter we adopt a different perspective from that taken up to now in this book, and look at how the 1983 Act has been implemented in terms of the equity of the experience of people in different circumstances and with different characteristics. The first question we have to ask is: who is being referred for consideration of action under the legislation, and second, are the outcomes of such referrals different for different groups of people? Our purpose here is twofold: to explore evidence about the extent to which mental disorder is experienced or identified more frequently amongst different groups, and then to look at any evidence of different responses to these groups once they have come to the attention of mental health professionals.

Ray Cochrane (Cochrane, 1983:3) has said that 'fluctuations in the incidence of disorders over time, place and social category are too large ever to be explained away by the differential incidence of some purely biochemical imbalance', and that understanding of the social context in which mental disorder is experienced is crucial to the development of resources that go beyond mere palliative measures. We suggest that understanding of the social construction of mental illness is insufficiently developed in the professional training of those most likely to adopt a social analysis of mental disorder. Social workers have failed to develop a language and intervention to reflect the social analysis they may be expected to proffer. Nor have they been sufficiently aware of the way in which their professional practice may reinforce dominant social ideologies affecting the identification and definition of mental disorder.

There is a complex interaction between factors such as: departmental policy (either explicit or implicit) regarding the availability of different types of service for people in different situations; social worker ideology; more general social assumptions about the nature and origins of mental disorder; and gender, age and racial stereotypes.

These will influence interactions between the social worker undertaking assessments under the Mental Health Act, 1983 and the person being assessed. Our project was not designed to explore how the interplay of such factors affected the outcomes for individuals, but at an aggregate level we can look for patterns that are indicative of the way in which they affect practice and thus the experience of those referred under the legislation.

Because there is no linear relationship between the four factors, it is not possible to discuss each under separate and distinct headings. For the purposes of ordering this discussion, we will take gender and living group, age, and race as our headings, and consider how general social assumptions about appropriate behaviour and roles are interpreted in the specific context that is the concern of this study. Another variable likely to affect outcome is psychiatric diagnosis. We will give less prominence to this partly because of our interest in looking at social variables, but also because we are less confident about the robustness of this variable. The social worker recording the diagnosis was repeating or interpreting medical diagnoses that often appeared rather vague.

Decisions about how to group people for the purpose of this analysis are to some extent arbitrary and dependent on our initial definition of the data collected about people's personal and social circumstances. Yet there is sufficient previous research evidence and evidence from the experience of those working with people with mental health problems to indicate that the variables we have chosen are central to an understanding of different experiences of mental disorder. The missing variable in this context is class. We did not feel confident that our method of data collection would enable us to obtain accurate information about the social class of people referred, nor that surrogate indicators (for example, housing tenure) would be sufficiently sensitive in this context.

In Chapter 4 we have pointed out the likely influence of local policy and practice on the outcomes of assessments for compulsory detention under different sections of the Act. For the purposes of the analysis in this chapter we have included not only those incidents in which there was a request to assess for a particular section, but all assessments where there was a possible outcome of detention under the Act. In addition to requests for assessment for sections 2, 3, and 4, we also include the comparatively few requests to assess for guardianship and for assessments under section 136 (following removal by the police). We also include the more numerous incidents in which the referrer did not specify assessment for a particular section, or in which there was some uncertainty about whether use of the Act was required. By adopting this approach we can say something about the extent to which different groups of people were made subject to the terms of the Act once they had been brought to the attention of one of the agencies responsible for interpreting and applying them. We can go some way beyond discussing in which circumstances the criteria for the use of a particular section were being met, and raise questions about the equity of the experience of different groups. Such questions include equity of access to services, as well as comparative experiences of the social control function of mental health legislation.

We will consider the results obtained from our analysis in the context of other research concerned more explicitly with the sociology of mental disorder.

GENDER AND LIVING GROUP

Women

During the last year of her life, the great feminist theorist Mary Wollstonecraft worked on a novel intended as a companion piece to her political treatise 'A Vindication of the Rights of Woman'. Left unfinished at her death in 1797, *Maria; or The*

> *Wrongs of Woman* describes 'the misery and oppression peculiar
> to women, that arise out of the partial laws and customs of
> society'. Wollstonecraft's heroine, Maria, has been forced into a
> madhouse by her abusive husband, who wants control of her
> fortune and liberty to pursue his sexual adventures. To Maria,
> the 'mansion of despair' in which she is incarcerated becomes
> a symbol of all the man-made institutions, from marriage to the
> law, that confine women and drive them mad. Listening to the
> songs and cries of the other women in the madhouse, Maria
> feels her own mind giving way. Yet she can find no reason to
> fight for her sanity or her freedom: 'was not the world a vast
> prison, and women born slaves?'

(Showalter, 1987:1)

So starts *The Female Malady:* by Elaine Showalter, subtitled *Women,
Madness and English Culture, 1830–1980*. In rather more evocative
ways, it is a book that explores the point made in a range of
statistical analyses that more women than men are defined as
suffering from mental illness. (See, for example, Figures 2.1 and
2.2 in Chapter 2, which detail comparative admissions to hospital.)

Our results confirm that women were, more often than men,
the subjects of assessments that could lead to the use of
compulsory detention or to other action under the legislation. In
this study, 5,315 women were involved in the incidents reported
compared with 4,090 men. This is not just a function of the over-
representation of women in the adult population. Our calculations
reveal that women in the authorities included in this study were
referred at a rate of 82.5 per 100,000 adult population, compared
with 68.4 per 100,000 men. And in terms of outcomes, a higher
proportion of the women assessed ended up by being compulsorily
detained in hospital: 52 per cent of women compared with 50 per
cent of men, a figure that mirrors DHSS figures for admissions.
These calculations are based on an analysis that includes all ethnic
groups in the study. In the section on race we will discuss evidence
that suggests that the over-representation of women compared
with men may be a particularly white phenomenon. There have
been cross-cultural studies of depression that show that a slightly
higher proportion of men than women suffered from symptoms of
depression (Carstairs and Kapur, 1976) and Fernando (1986).
This suggests that the male-female difference is likely to be a

cultural phenomenon related to the status of men and women within the community. The discussion that follows assumes gender differences associated with Western European cultures.

The DHSS figures quoted earlier (Chapter 2) also reveal something of the difference in circumstances of men and women admitted to hospital under mental health legislation. They show that the risk of admission for men and women varies according to age. If we look more closely at our results we find considerable differences in the circumstances of the men and women referred to social workers for assessment. Not only were there important differences in age, there were also considerable differences in living group and marital status, which suggest that it is not just differences in absolute numbers or rates of women referred that ought to concern us. Table 6.1 highlights the key differences. (See Appendix 5 for more detailed information about the comparative circumstances of the men and women referred.)

Table 6.1 Circumstances of men and women

Circumstances	Men %	Women %
Single	55.8	28.6
Married	24.5	34.1
Living alone	30.0	33.4
In lodgings or homeless	12.0	5.7
Living with spouse or cohabitee	24.3	33.7
Living with parents	26.2	11.2
Under 35	44.8	27.8
Over 65	13.4	25.5

The difference in marital status between men and women is outstanding. Men were more likely to come to the attention of a social worker for action under the mental health legislation if they were single than if they were married. The position for women is reversed. The small difference in the proportion of men and women living on their own conceals substantial differences within these populations. Over 40 per cent of women living on their own were elderly, whereas men living on their own were much more likely to be in the 25–44 age group. More than twice as many men than women were living in lodgings or were homeless and men were also slightly more likely to be living in residential accommodation provided by statutory health and social services or by private and voluntary agencies.

131

Overall, women were more likely to be living in what is regarded as the normal circumstance for adults. They were more likely to be living with a partner of their own generation in accommodation that was personal to them. Men, on the other hand, were less likely to have broken away from their family of birth and less likely to have forged partnerships that led to the creation of new households of their own. This is partly to do with age – more of the men referred were young adults, whereas women were more often middle-aged or elderly. But the fact remains that amongst those referred to social workers in need of assessment because of mental health problems, more women than men were in situations that would not normally be regarded as indicative of risk.

Why is it that men apparently exhibiting the signs of some form of mental disorder are more likely also to be in some other way 'deviant' than are women? Possible explanations for this can be found in other research evidence. The fact of women's more frequent involvement with psychiatric services and more frequent receipt of prescriptions for psychotropic drugs is not in dispute (see Fransella and Frost, 1977). There is much dispute over the reason for this, and over how such a fact should be interpreted. At the root of this is the definition of normal, healthy, adult behaviour. Research by Broverman (Broverman *et al.*, 1970) has demonstrated that behaviour defined as 'male' is seen by psychiatrists to be congruent with healthy behaviour, whilst behaviour defined as 'female' is not. Healthy women were considered to be more submissive, less independent, less adventurous, more easily influenced, less aggressive, less competitive, more excitable in minor crises, having their feelings more easily hurt, being more emotional, more conceited about their appearance, and less objective than were healthy men. This assessment of women is couched in primarily negative terms and is evidence that healthy women were perceived to be less healthy than men. Other evidence of dual standards is found in the work of Fabrikant (1974) who reported that 'male therapists rated 70 per cent of female concepts as negative whereas they rated 71 per cent of male concepts as positive' (quoted in Fransella and Frost, 1977: 187).

Similar perceptions amongst the general population were described by Jones and Cochrane (1981). They found that there was a much greater similarity in the concepts chosen to describe a mentally ill woman and a normal woman, than there was in concepts chosen to describe a mentally ill man and a normal man. Using a series of scales determined by adjectives indicating opposite characteristics: e.g. 'outgoing–withdrawn', 'sensitive–insensitive', 'irritable–calm', and 'pleasant–unpleasant', they found that there was a clear differentiation in the adjectives chosen to describe a mentally ill man from those chosen to describe a normal man. However, there was much less difference in the descriptions of a mentally ill woman and a normal woman.

Mental disorder is one form of deviance recognized by society; criminality is another. The picture painted by criminal statistics suggests fundamental differences in the way in which deviance is defined according to gender. As Barrett and McIntosh note:

> There are two striking, though crude, statistical facts that demand an explanation. One is that far more men than women are convicted of criminal offences; another is that more women than men are treated for depressive and neurotic mental illness. Though the processes involved are far from clear, it is hard to resist the conclusion that these correlations are in some way rooted in men's and women's different relation to private and public life.
>
> (Barrett and McIntosh, 1982:58)

This may suggest that the dominant definition of mental ill health, which appears to relate this to female rather than male characteristics, serves to ignore the mental health problems of men who become labelled as 'criminal' rather than 'ill'. It may be that men are being deprived of the potential benefits of mental health services because they themselves are less likely to identify their problems in terms of mental distress and to seek help for them in those terms.

The relationship between externally imposed definitions of the meanings of particular types of behaviour, and the source of such behaviour in the individual's response to her experience of her social world, is extremely hard to unravel. The best that we can do in this analysis is to point to aspects of women's experience that could account for the greater prevalence of mental disorder, particularly depression, amongst women, but also to point out that the definitions of such behaviour are not gender neutral and themselves have to be understood in the social context in which they were formulated.

By definition, then, women's behaviour is more likely to put them at risk of receiving a psychiatric diagnosis. But this is not the only reason for their over-representation in mental health statistics. An American study by Roth and Lerner found that:

> Approximately three times as many women as men have received psychosurgery. The claim that psychosurgery has sometimes been used on women primarily to push women into traditional caring roles is supported by the overt statements of certain psychosurgeons, one of whom observed that after a lobotomy 'some women do the dishes better, are better housewives and comply with the sexual demands of their husbands . . . it takes away their aggressiveness.
>
> (Roth and Lerner, 1974, quoted in Dale and Foster, 1986)

In quoting this example we are not assuming that psychosurgery is a usual response to women (or men) who are experiencing mental health problems. We also acknowledge that the Mental Health Act, 1983 includes provisions designed to ensure that its use is limited. But what it does demonstrate is the existence of an attitude amongst certain sections of the psychiatric profession that was evident comparatively recently and that made explicit the way in which psychiatry can be used to maintain women in the female role of wife, mother, and housekeeper. It is a response based on the definition of what is 'proper' behaviour for a woman, and it is a blatant example of psychiatry as control.

Women may still find themselves subject to more subtle forms of control from a psychiatric profession that too often views mental distress in women as a result of their resistance to their feminine role. This starts with the GP who is most likely to be the first point of contact for those with mental health problems.

> Research has shown, for example, that women patients are far more likely to be labelled as neurotic or over emotional by their doctors. Two British sociologists have made an interesting comparison of their treatment for migraine. Whereas David Oldman, a family man with a high powered job, never encountered any suggestion that his way of life was responsible for his attacks, Sally MacIntyre, as a single research student, was

told that her migraine resulted from her not having a boyfriend and from her sublimation of her desire to have children.

(MacIntyre and Oldman, 1977:62 quoted in Dale and Foster, 1986:94)

Similarly Goldberg and Huxley (1980) provide evidence of the differential rate at which doctors consider patients to be suffering from psychological as opposed to physical problems. They found doctors less likely to identify psychological problems if the patient is *male*, very young or over 65, unmarried, or better educated.

If the 'diagnosis' of the origins of mental stress in women locates this in a rejection of their 'true nature' then the 'treatment' is seen to lie in finding ways to encourage her back into an acceptable role. In discussing other research that looked at social services involvement in cases where both mental health problems and child-care problems were seen to coexist, we noted that it was more likely to be the child-care aspects of the 'case' that were addressed, whilst the mother's mental distress was not (Fisher *et al.*, 1984). This suggests that social work gives greater emphasis to preserving the family than it does to exploring and addressing the distress women may experience in the role of mother.

Others have looked at the content of social work practice with women with severe mental health problems and found evidence of sexist practice that has been detrimental to the women concerned (see, for example, Davis *et al.*, 1985; GLC, 1985). This extract from a social work case file quoted by Judy Hale illustrates how social workers can blame women for not fulfilling their expected role:

> Inadequate manipulative woman whose tendency to depression leads her to neglect her home and family. In spite of a supportive husband she does not seem able to function in her role as wife and mother although there has been no success in persuading her not to have more children.

(Hale, 1983: 171)

If women are more likely to be referred for assessment following a preliminary identification of mental health problems (by a GP, for example), are they then likely to experience different outcomes from men in a similar situation? We looked at the different outcomes following assessment for possible action under the Mental Health Act for men and women of different ages and in a number of different circumstances. We compared outcomes for single men and women living with their parents, for men and women under 54 years old who were living with a spouse or cohabitee (with or without children), for young men and women under the age of 35, for 'middle aged' men and women who were aged between 35 and 64, and for men and women who were living on their own. With the exception of the young women aged under 35, women in each of these groups were more likely to be compulsorily detained in hospital following a social work assessment than were the men. In some cases the statistical difference was small (see Appendix 6 for exact figures), but nevertheless our results confirm other observations that from middle age onwards, women are more likely than are men to be on the receiving end of psychiatric compulsion.

Where hospital admission was not the outcome, there were also differences in the alternatives used. Residential care was a rarely used option for all groups, but it was used least frequently as an alternative to admission for middle-aged women. It was used in only 4 per cent of cases in which admission of women aged 35–64 was avoided compared with its use in 8 per cent of such instances overall. It was also rarely seen to be appropriate as an alternative to hospital admission for middle-aged women. Entering hospital can be legitimated by 'being ill' and 'needing treatment'. It will involve temporary disruption to family life and arrangements may need to be made for the care of children whilst mother is away. In extreme cases this may involve a temporary reception into care. But moving to other accommodation, which cannot be seen as a place where a cure for an illness can be found, is more challenging. If the family is seen as the fount of succour and the place where its members seek nurturing, why does one of its members who is not sick need to move elsewhere for support? The following quotation from a woman attending a mental health centre provides a clue to this:

> I was taking on so much of the worry of all the family. Our house was like the citizen's advice bureau. I wanted to scream 'Shut up! You are upsetting me,' but the scream stayed there; it wouldn't come out.
>
> (Bailey, 1987:30)

Overall, family support was used in 47 per cent of cases in which women's admission to hospital was prevented, compared with 39 per cent of cases involving men. The family was more often used as a source of support to prevent the admission of women to hospital than it was to prevent men being admitted. This applies to women of different age groups and different ethnic groups. It applies to women living alone, to single women living with their parents, to middle-aged women living with a partner. The only circumstance in which family support for men more often prevented hospital admission than it did for women was in relation to men already living in some form of residential accommodation.

So although our results concerning living circumstances at time of referral suggest that the family might more often provide a safe haven for men than women, it is nevertheless more often the case that women are those referred back to the family for help. And in those cases where social workers thought hospital admission could have been prevented, they were again identifying family support as a resource to prevent admission more frequently in relation to women of all ages, ethnic groups, and living circumstances. The emphasis on the domestic sphere as the proper place for women and the place in which their mental health can be revived was being reinforced both in practice and in preference.

If women are bearing the heaviest load in *providing* the nurturing for the rest of the family, and if women themselves have learnt that this is what they should be doing, to admit that such a role is a source of distress and can result in mental health problems for the woman herself seriously undermines some of society's most cherished beliefs about the nature of families. It can also produce dilemmas for the women concerned when they seek help:

> Most housewives and mothers who consult their GP complaining of severe tiredness, anxiety or depression are 'treated' with tranquillizers and anti-depressants. In the early 1980s one woman in five compared to one man in ten was taking tranquillizers at some time during the course of a year. Major drug companies' advertisements have told GPs that tranquillizers or anti-depressants are the solution to problems such as women living in high rise flats (Tristafen), women being unable to choose between goods in a supermarket (Prothiaden), female students under stress (Tranxiene) and the boredom of housework (Limbitrol).
>
> (Dale and Foster, 1986:92)

Whilst we would not hesitate to recognize the qualitative difference between psychosurgery and the prescription of anti-depressants, the similar origins of such responses to women unable to cope with their assigned roles must be obvious. A social response (and thus the response that should be available from social services departments) should include the option of changing the social circumstances out of which mental health problems have grown. In saying this we are not advocating the provision of alternative accommodation for all women whose family circumstances are causing stress or depression. We *are* suggesting that social workers may need to address specifically the role of the women who are referred to them with mental health problems and decide whether individual, family, or group therapy might address some of the underlying problems, or whether more practical solutions such as providing help with child care, assistance in finding a job, or rehousing might be called for. Our reading of descriptions of the circumstances leading to referral and of the possible outcomes proposed provides little evidence that such questions receive explicit attention, or if they do, that appropriate resources are available to address them.

In addition to stress associated with difficulties of adapting to expected gender roles, a number of factors have been identified that can affect women's mental health. Research by Seligman (1975) has suggested that depression can be a consequence of a low capacity to influence the environment. Married women, dependent on their husbands for financial support, often having their geographical location determined by the requirements of his job, are more likely to feel unable to influence their environment than are single, financially independent women. In the study by Brown and Harris (1978) of depression in working-class women, not having paid employment outside the home was identified as one of the factors making some women more vulnerable to depression than others. This finding was confirmed by Cochrane and Stopes-Roe (1981) who found that having paid employment reduced the number of symptoms of depression reported by married women. Less than 6 per cent of the women referred during our study were in full-time paid employment, and only 4.4 per cent were in part-time employment.

Whilst we did not carry out a complete analysis of the descriptions of circumstances leading to referral that were provided by the social workers in this study, our perusal of a random selection from the monitoring forms gives little indication that factors such as these were at the forefront of workers' awareness when they were assessing the people referred to them. There was little exploration of those aspects of women's situations that might be causing or exacerbating their mental health problems compared with references to psychiatric diagnoses or women's 'failure to co-operate' with treatment. Admittedly, we asked for only brief descriptions of the circumstances leading to referral, but in this situation the dominance of medical or psychiatric analyses over social analyses is even more marked. If workers *were* aware of the significance of social factors this was not often demonstrated in their descriptions. We could speculate that they do not have the language with which to describe apparently abnormal behaviour in terms other than those adopted in psychiatry. Thus the tendency appeared to be to provide a statement of the immediate situation with reference to apparent delusions and concern for physical wellbeing. The following description may serve as an example. It relates to a married white woman of 41, living with her children and involved in full-time care of her home and family. No psychiatric diagnosis was recorded:

> Client very suspicious believing husband wished to kill her and the children – making children lie on the floor to avoid shooting. Very manic and erratic. Ideas about the house being bugged by FBI agents, hallucinating, not eating, making 'unrealistic' demands on children.

She was referred for an unspecified assessment and admitted under section 2. Suggested alternatives to admission were support from family, neighbours, and her GP:

> Alternatives used for a few days – when neighbourhood support was withdrawn, compulsory admission was necessary.

We cannot help but feel that the social workers providing descriptions such as this did not have the confidence to confront aspects of the social situations that could have marked impact on the mental health of the women concerned. In giving prominence to medical factors in this as in other cases, they failed to propose alternative explanations and thus alternative solutions. Perhaps because they knew that such referrals would receive little priority in terms of attracting continuing support from the social services department, perhaps because their training had not given them the skills to address directly the mental distress of clients such as these women, they concentrated on the symptoms of that distress and on ensuring immediate safety from the effect of those symptoms.

Living groups

Our study has shown that the typical circumstances of men and women referred for action under the legislation were different. Women were more likely to be wives and mothers than were men to be husbands and fathers. The conclusion that family life is protective of men's mental health, but destructive of women's, is too simplistic, but our evidence does support other work that points to difficulties for women in negotiating a family role congruent with their individual needs.

Other evidence points to the fact that family life may not be an unambiguous source of care and support. Our previous discussion of the importance of supportive networks might have suggested that people living alone would be most at risk of compulsory admission and that it would be most difficult to develop or support caring networks for people without the immediate support of cohabitees. In fact this group were amongst those least likely to be compulsorily detained and were the group second most likely to receive alternative care out of hospital. This appears to conflict with the findings of a study by Szmukler *et al.* (1981) in Camden. This showed that, compared with informally admitted patients, compulsorily admitted patients showed greater social dislocation (defined by a number of variables, including living alone) than did informally admitted patients. One reason for our findings was that many of those living alone were elderly and, as we shall see below, elderly people were generally less likely to be admitted than are younger people, although Gilleard (1985) quotes research that suggests that social isolation does seem to contribute to hospital admission amongst elderly people. Another suggestion that draws some strength from work previously quoted in Chapter 2 is that a factor contributing to the likelihood of hospital admission is the exclusion of people with mental disorder from cohabiting groups. Those living on their own may be able to behave in ways that would not be accepted by others living in immediate contact with them and thus are able to express their individuality without causing immediate harm or concern that could result in the attraction of a label of mental disorder. Looking at the same situation in a rather different way, those living alone may have no-one to advocate on their behalf and seek the care and treatment that hospital admission could provide.

Nevertheless, social workers felt that a higher proportion of those living alone compared with all other groups who were admitted to hospital could have avoided this option if other sources of support had been available. Often, as was the case with other groups, social workers were looking to families to provide more help. But they also identified resources such as day care, which could be a source both of companionship and monitoring, and suggested that 41 per cent of men living alone and 33 per cent of women could have been found alternative residential accommodation. This is a very different picture from that provided by the resources actually used. Residential care was an alternative to hospital admission in only 7 per cent of cases involving women and 8 per cent involving men. Support from social workers was by far the most frequent resource used in these circumstances.

The experience of people living in National Health Service, social services, voluntary, or private accommodation could be viewed as the polar opposite of those living alone. One might assume that they are already in an environment in which a high level of support could be provided. Specifically staff could ensure that required medication was taken regularly, that there would be the opportunity for group or individual therapy, the development of crises might be prevented as changes in behaviour started to become evident, and that the stresses associated with having to deal with the practicalities of daily life at times of emotional distress would be minimized by the buffer of group living. Yet people referred from these living environments were more likely to be compulsorily detained than those living on their own. In practice terms we have to ask whether this represents a failure on the part of those institutions and whether it implies that putting too strong an emphasis on alternative residential accommodation as a means of preventing hospital admission is mistaken. People already living in institutional environments are conceivably those whose mental disorder is interfering more with their ability to maintain an independent existence than is the case for those living alone. It may also be the case that their problems can be contained for longer so that referral is made when a more extreme solution is required. Certainly the numbers involved were considerably smaller. But we think it is important to stress that alternative accommodation *per se*, at least as it is currently provided, is not necessarily a permanent alternative to hospital admission.

Not surprisingly, family support was proportionately a much-less-frequent alternative to hospital admission for those already living in some form of residential accommodation. Yet it did feature in approximately one-fifth of cases where hospital admission was avoided. What is not clear is whether this involved a move from such accommodation into family care, or whether families were called in to play a more active role in supporting the person in the home or hostel. Voluntary help featured more often in such circumstances than in relation to people living in their own or family homes, and as in most other cases, support from social workers, GPs, and community psychiatric nurses featured in a substantial proportion of cases. What this suggests is that these additional elements in the support network are equally important when people experiencing mental health problems are living in residential care as when they are living at home.

Men and Mental Disorder

Research focusing specifically on men's experience of mental distress is rare. The identification of mental health with predominantly male rather than female characteristics may suggest why this should be so and we have quoted from Barrett and McIntosh (1982) the observation that deviance amongst men is more often defined as criminality than madness. Our major argument in the previous section was that mental distress amongst women is often a result of stresses associated with stereotypical assumptions about gender roles. The same problems are not experienced by men. The influential work of Brown and Harris (1978) provides convincing evidence that women experience depression following a serious life event if certain predisposing factors are present – having three or more children under 14 years of age living at home, being unemployed, losing one's mother in childhood, and lacking an intimate, confiding relationship. Any of these factors *could* be a part of men's experience and yet their study did not look at men's responses in comparable situations. Thus there is the risk that the findings can be interpreted as evidence of female pathology that predisposes women to depression.

One of the 'predisposing factors' identified by Brown and Harris (1978) – being unemployed – has provided the basis for some of the few studies that have considered mental health problems in men. The starting point of such studies is unemployment rather than mental distress and thus they can provide only a partial analysis of the male experience of mental disorder.

Historically, mental ill-health amongst men has been a dilemma for those who equate male characteristics with desirable adult behaviour. It took the major upheaval of the First World War and the reactions of thousands of young, healthy men who experienced shell shock to challenge the assumption amongst psychiatrists that hysteria was an exclusively female phenomenon. Psychiatrists in the late nineteenth and early twentieth centuries documented many cases of female hysteria. Freud is the most famous of these, but was not the first to describe and characterize hysteria as a female affliction. Elaine Showalter describes the French psychiatrist Jean-Martin Charcot as the first great European theorist of hysteria. He linked hysteria to female sexuality and maintained that the ovarian region of the body might produce convulsions when pressed.

However, the identification of hysteria as a 'fin du siecle epidemic of female nervous disorder' (Showalter, 1987: 64) was undermined when the symptoms of shell shock amongst the 80,000 men passing through army medical facilities during the course of the war were observed to be very similar. At first it was thought that the physical force or chemical effects of shells bursting close to the men had caused the loss of sensory capabilities and, in some cases, loss of memory from which they were suffering. But on examination, no physical cause could be found, and indeed, some of the sufferers had not even been under fire. The realization that what was becoming evident was the emergence of 'male hysteria' not only produced a fundamental challenge to the assumptions on which late nineteenth century psychiatry had been based, it also challenged much more general assumptions about manly behaviour: 'This parade of emotionally incapacitated men was in itself a shocking contrast to the heroic visions and masculinist fantasies that had preceded it' (Showalter, 1987:169). Mental distress as demonstrated amongst these young men was a form of gender betrayal, made most explicit in the sexual impotence of many experiencing the disabling effects of war.

This may provide us with some understanding of why mental health problems are more frequently evident at the time of young adulthood in men. If the obverse of the characteristics reported by Broverman *et al.* (1970) as characteristic of healthy adult women are considered characteristic of healthy adult men, those young men who do not experience themselves as dominant, independent, adventurous, aggressive, and competitive may experience crises at the time in their lives when they are expected to break away from their family of birth and make their own way in the world. Certainly evidence of the age of onset of schizophrenia (the most frequent diagnosis for the young men in our study) would suggest a link with the transition to adult identity. Schizophrenia is most frequently diagnosed in late adolescence or early adulthood. Unpublished work by Lu (Lu, 1970 quoted in Lu, 1985) looking at American schizophrenic patients 'indicates that their major role strains center on their inability to cope with the demands or high social expectations for achievement, independence and work performance.'

Our analysis of outcomes for people in different living groups provides findings of relevance in this context. Of all the groups we looked at it was clear that it was single men and women living with their parents who were most likely to be compulsorily detained following assessment. Here we have to make a distinction between numbers and percentages. In absolute terms more men than women were in this situation and virtually twice as many men than women living with their parents were compulsorily detained. However, a higher *proportion* of women than men in this situation were made subject to a compulsory detention.

Why should this be so? Whilst this project can offer no direct evidence relating to cause and effect, we can suggest that adults who have not broken away from their family of birth are likely to be those who find it most difficult to develop networks that provide both support and confirmation of their status as a valued adult. For whatever reason, women are more likely to make this transition than are men, and those who do not may be those whose difficulties are most severe. The protectiveness of parents and their ability to provide unconditional care may mean that problems are absorbed most of the time, and when a referral is made it is usually because of recognition of the signs of periodic deterioration, or because a crisis has erupted that is too serious to contain within the home environment. An example of this kind of situation is suggested by the following example taken from one of the monitoring forms:

> Said to have been aggressive and violent, smashing up his room, breaking window, threatening mother, shouting abuse to passers-by outside the front door. Mother feared for her own safety as well as her younger children. G. (client) refused to go to hospital. Query drug abuse.

Nevertheless, young men living in the parental home were more likely to avoid hospital admission as a result of family support than men in any of the other situations we looked at. If the origins of schizophrenia (the most frequent diagnosis of young men) are thought to have some relationship to communication patterns in families, it could be more appropriate in many situations to seek alternative accommodation with the necessary support than to maintain the existing family group. Residential accommodation was used to avoid admission in only 10 (5.4 per cent) instances relating to single men living with their parents. The problem lies both in finding appropriate and affordable accommodation for young men who may have previously failed to achieve independence and who are very likely to be unemployed, and to provide a social network that can ensure that independence does not mean isolation. Social workers did feel that alternative residential accommodation was a potentially important resource. They felt it would have prevented hospital admission in 41 per cent of instances concerning single men living with their parents, where admission was considered avoidable. It was the most frequently identified potential alternative for this group.

Evidence of the link between mental health problems and the experience of unemployment amongst men provides further confirmation that the source of mental ill-health can be in the dissonance between an individual perception of self, and a social definition of what is proper behaviour for a man. (In this discussion we are not implying that unemployment has no consequence for women in terms of their mental health. Indeed, we have already indicated that paid employment is an important source of psychological wellbeing for women. We are instead focusing on generally held assumptions about gender roles that we consider can be experienced as a source of stress by both women *and* men.)

Peter Leonard introduces his discussion of *Marginality in the Social Order* with a definition of the problem that has great resonance here:

> The problem which we must tackle from a materialist perspective is this: production and social reproduction are central to the social order and to the individual's identity within it. Ideological discourse is directed from childhood onwards to the performance of the productive and reproductive roles which gendered class subjects are expected to perform. Familial ideology is especially significant in constructing a self which is congruent with dominant conceptions of the activities and capacities involved in present or future roles: mother, father, bread-winner, 'attractive young woman', 'useful member of society' and others. But what happens to those who do not appear to occupy these central roles? What is the effect of subordinate marginality on personality?
>
> (Leonard, 1984:181)

A number of studies of unemployed people provide some of the answers to that question. Hayes and Nutman (1981) have produced a model demonstrating the transitional stages that people go through following job loss. After an initial period of immobilization, a period of making light of the problem can produce an increase in self-esteem. However, as time goes on and no new job is found, depression starts to set in and self-esteem to dive. The downward path can be halted with the acceptance of the reality of the new situation and over time a search for and internalization of new meanings can lead to a potential increase in self-esteem. The up-curve is evidence of a coming to terms with a new life-style embodying new attitudes and behaviours and a new acceptance of self. As with any ideal type, this model does not describe the process for everyone experiencing redundancy and in the context of this study we are concerned with those people who are not able to move into the up-curve but continue on the downward path of depression.

It is perhaps best to hear from unemployed people themselves of the effect unemployment has on their mental health:

> I don't think there's a stigma to it . . . .it's the person themselves feels there's a stigma to it . . . . They feel it themselves.
>
> (Coxall, 1987:30)

> I think the family started disintegrating then. I started to drink too much, getting into vicious tempers, I was easily angry and upset and I used to snap at the children all the time. I started having these deep depressions and nobody could help me.
>
> (Fagin, 1981:63)

> When you're unemployed, you feel like you've committed a crime somewhere, but nobody tells you what you've done. The first thing that happened to me was that I realised I'd become almost illiterate after years working in a factory. I fall asleep a lot, it happens if you've got nothing to do. One bloke round here, the only place he goes is to sign on the dole. Sometimes I think I'll go barmy. Of course, you get depressed, you convince yourself it's you.
>
> (Campbell, 1984:179)

A combination of resulting financial hardship, lack of time structure, lack of social contacts, and lack of purpose means that unemployment undermines the structure on which most (male) adult lives are built. Underlying all this is the fact that an individual's very identity is determined primarily by the role they occupy in the productive sphere. People define themselves and are defined by others by the work they do. Without that reference point, self-doubt can lead to a crisis in mental health. Unemployed men experience both ambivalence and difficulty in taking on nurturing and domestic roles within the family because the nurturing aspects of personality are not normally seen to be consistent with masculine personality. In some cases attempts to change roles within the family can result in considerable disruption because of expectations about appropriate and non-appropriate gender behaviour:

> Phil's self-image, based primarily on the nature of his job was

147

beginning to show serious cracks when he did not have a breadwinning role to play. Wyn was beginning to realise that she had to rely on all her strength rather than be dependent on Phil. There was tension, bitterness and sadness about these changes which neither felt able to control.

(Fagin, 1981:73)

This discussion can provide some understanding of the differences in the circumstances of the women and men experiencing severe mental health problems that have led to a referral for consideration of action under the Mental Health Act, 1983. We have noted that overall, women were slightly more likely to be admitted compulsorily to hospital following assessment than were men. However, if we subdivide the population there were three groups amongst which this picture was reversed: young men under 35 and Afro-Caribbean and Asian men were compulsorily detained more often than women in these groups. We will consider the influence of race on the experience of the mental health legislation in the next section. The difference in outcomes for young men and women is small and is probably accounted for by the concentration of black men in the younger age groups. However, it does re-emphasize the way in which gender interacts with age in influencing outcomes.

Again, when hospital admission was avoided and some form of alternative care was provided, decisions as to what that care should consist of reflected gender distinctions. Men in all the groups we looked at were less likely to receive support from family or neighbours. In proportionate terms, this was least likely for men between the ages of 35 and 64 and for Asian men. Overall they were more likely to receive day care, be referred for out-patients appointments, and to receive help from voluntary agencies than were women, but less likely to receive support from individual professionals: social workers, GPs, CPNs, and domiciliary-care workers, or to receive residential care. This overall pattern remains largely consistent, with the exception that middle-aged men were slightly less likely than middle-aged women to be referred for out-patient appointments and slightly more likely to be found alternative residential accommodation.

We have already noted that in those circumstances where men *were* admitted to hospital, but the social workers providing the assessment felt that admission could have been prevented, family support was less often seen as a means of preventing admission than it was in the case of women. Perhaps as a corollary of this, alternative residential accommodation was more often viewed as a preventive resource for most of the subgroups of men than women. The exceptions were in the case of single men living with their parents, men under 54 living with a partner, and Asian men (but the numbers involved in the latter comparison are very small).

It is not possible to separate out questions about the different rates at which mental disorder is experienced from questions of professional response to those defined as being mentally disordered. Definition itself determines what is to be counted. The nearest one can get to an objective count of the prevalence of mental disorder in different sections of the population are studies that use standardized questionnaires such as the Langner 22-Item Scale (see Cochrane, 1983) with samples drawn from the population at large. Yet such methods are not sensitive to extreme forms of mental disorder and conversely identify large numbers of people who may never come to the attention of professionals for assistance to deal with their problems. By agreeing that someone should be compulsorily detained in hospital under the Mental Health Act, 1983, an approved social worker is confirming that in her/his opinion that person is mentally disordered under the terms of the Act, and that help cannot be provided to them outside hospital. They are thus contributing to the categorization of certain types of behaviour as indicative of 'mental illness, arrested or incomplete development of mind, psychopathic disorder' (Mental Health Act, 1983, section 1(2)). Our two questions posed at the beginning of this chapter, concerning the frequency with which mental disorder is experienced by different groups, and the different experiences of people in different circumstances and with different characteristics once they come to the attention of mental health professionals, cannot be posed or answered independently of each other.

Our purpose in discussing this question in some detail in the context of this study is to do three things: first, to alert social workers to some of the potential sources of mental distress in the women and men they are called on to assess for compulsory hospital detention, second, to encourage workers to be aware of responses based on stereotypical assumptions of appropriate gender roles, and third, to suggest to those responsible for resource and policy decision-making in social services departments that legitimate concern over child-care issues should not crowd out space to work in appropriate ways with the parents of those children when they are at risk.

Our results suggest that, however unintentionally, social workers are reinforcing gender stereotypes by failing to draw sufficiently on the body of knowledge that locates both the definition and experience of mental disorder in a social context. Working in an under-resourced and secondary mental health social service, their ability to challenge the 'scientific' knowledge of psychiatry is limited. But their role under the legislation, however constrained, is to provide an independent assessment. For that assessment to be truly independent it should not be based on borrowings from psychiatry, but derive from the skills of social workers in understanding how social pressures can affect individual behaviour, and how the relationship between the individual and her social world can be changed by practical assistance, therapeutic relationships, and temporary or more permanent removal from the source of stress.

AGE

Attempts to understand the social construction of old age have, until recently, received comparatively little attention from social-policy analysts and from those concerned to develop age-appropriate services. Consideration of how this affects elderly people's experiences of mental health problems is even rarer and there is much less material for us to draw on in our attempts to view our results in respect of elderly people in a specifically sociological context.

As with the re-emergence of unemployment as a fundamental structural factor affecting large numbers of people who are recipients of welfare services, the very fact of both absolute and proportional increases in the numbers of elderly people in the population has forced a reconsideration of the adequacy of services designed for elderly people. In doing so it has become necessary to consider why old age is both perceived and, in many cases experienced, as a problem. The needs of increasing numbers of elderly mentally infirm people are resulting in strains both on professional services and personal carers.

Early on in our analysis it became clear that a considerable number of those people being referred for action under the legislation were elderly. We highlighted this in our initial feedback to participants, expressing some surprise and concern at the fact that over one-fifth of those referred were over 65. That proportion remained constant throughout the year during which data was collected, resulting in a final total of 1,903 people over 65 years of age being referred for consideration of action under the legislation – 20.3 per cent of the total referred. Whilst the Act makes no specific reference to its appropriateness (or otherwise) in the case of elderly people, the Mental Health Act Commission did single out elderly people as a group for whom compulsory admission should be avoided if at all possible. Hence our concern at the numbers who were being *considered* for possible detention.

The over-representation of women amongst those being considered under the terms of the Mental Health Act is particularly marked amongst elderly people. More than twice as many elderly women as men were referred during the year we studied – 1,356 compared with 547, and the proportion of women to men increased the older they were (see Figure 6.1).

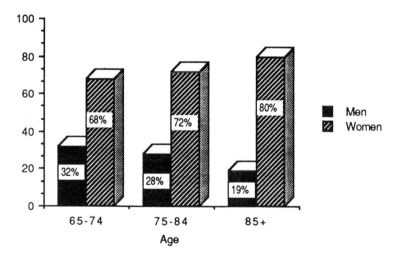

Figure 6.1 Gender of elderly people referred

Once again this is not a function of the gender distribution within the elderly population. The higher rate at which elderly women were referred compared with elderly men was more marked than amongst the population as a whole. Elderly women were referred at a rate of 92.2 per 100,000, compared with 56.3 per 100,000 men. The larger number of very elderly women is reflected in the fact that a much higher proportion of women than men were widowed – 56 per cent of women whose marital status was known were widowed compared with 29 per cent of men. The figures are reversed for those still married as nearly half (49 per cent) of elderly men were married compared with less than one-quarter of the women (23 per cent). Depression following bereavement might be expected to be a more common feature of the experience of the elderly women who are coming to the attention of social services departments in this context. However, there was no difference in the proportions of elderly men and women who had a diagnosis of depression. Also somewhat surprisingly, the proportion of elderly men who had a diagnosis of dementia was slightly higher than that of women – 32 per cent compared with 29 per cent. The reverse might have been expected in view of the age structure of the two groups.

Another feature of the diagnostic characteristics of the elderly men and women was that schizophrenia appeared more often as a diagnosis of elderly women than of elderly men. There is a subsidiary peak in the onset of schizophrenia at 75-plus and it has been demonstrated elsewhere that 4 per cent of all schizophrenic illnesses in men and 14 per cent in women occur after the age of 65. (Kay, 1963)

The living circumstances of elderly men and women were very different from each other and from those of the younger groups referred. Of men aged 65 or more, 33 per cent were living alone, compared with 55 per cent of women in this age group. In contrast, 44 per cent of men were living with a spouse or cohabitee (with or without their children), whereas only 21 per cent of women were in this situation. In absolute numbers, women living alone made up by far the largest group within this section of the referred population.

The role reversal experienced in old age was reflected in the comparatively high proportion of those living with their children only who were in the 65-plus age group.

Whilst the current marital status of both elderly men and women was very different, the proportion who had at some stage in their lives been married was exactly the same. The differential impact of family life and the role conflict that appears to make married women more susceptible, and married men less suscept- ible to mental health problems cannot provide a similar explan- ation for the mental disorder experienced by many of the elderly people in our study. This may indicate that mental distress appeared late in life rather than being a continuation of mental health problems experienced when they were younger. Yet even in old age, the circumstances in which this distress was experienced still varied according to gender. Elderly women were more isolated in their living situations as well as having been more likely to have experienced loss. There is some indication that they were more likely to be experiencing forms of psychosis than were men, whilst the predominance of diagnoses of neuroses in earlier life no longer applied. The two diagnoses of senile dementia and depression account for 58.1 per cent of diagnoses of the elderly people included in the study (30.4 per cent and 27.7 per cent respectively).

What are the particular features of mental disorder in old age and how can they be understood in a way that will assist social workers involved in assessments to reach appropriate conclusions about outcomes? The organic nature of senile dementia means that both the origin and nature of the resultant mental distress are rather different from many other mental health problems experienced by those referred to social workers under the Mental Health Act, 1983. However, its manifestations in general will be influenced by the social circumstances of the person concerned.

Bernard Isaacs gives a clear example of how mental disorder is rarely the only problem to be experienced by elderly people.

The affective disorders rarely occur in isolation – usually they are accompanied by physical disease, by social loss and deprivation, by brain failure or by a combination of all three. For example, a woman of 84 suffered from severe anxiety and bouts of depression. She lived alone, had no relatives, had fallen repeatedly, and had lain all night on the floor on two occasions. Furthermore the house next door had been vandalized. She had apparently adequate reasons to feel anxious and depressed, and yet these feelings were persistent and persuasive and were judged to be abnormal. Her anxiety and depression improved with drug treatment even though the adverse physical and social factors persisted. It is possible, but unlikely, that she might have recovered equally well if she had been rehoused or given a course of physiotherapy and not received drugs. However, physical, social and psychiatric factors are so intertwined in the circumstances of many old people that an integrated approach to treatment is the one most likely to yield favourable results.

(Gray and Isaacs, 1979:31)

Depression can, perhaps, be most easily understood in terms of the way in which old age is defined and experienced in contemporary capitalist society. In Peter Leonard's discussion referred to in the previous section (p.146), old people are included within those defined as marginal, or more accurately as experiencing 'involuntary subordinate marginality', in view of their exclusion from the productive and reproductive activity of capitalism. The potential similarity to the experience of unemployed people is described by Leonard:

Apart from the financial crisis which many people face on retirement, elderly people, especially men, face a crisis of identity too. Men's identity, in particular, is often bound up with their wage labour role: the answer to the questions 'What are you?' or 'What do you do?' lies in describing one's paid work. For many elderly people, at least at the beginning of retirement, there is often an experience which could be described as mourning the loss of a 'productive role'.

(Leonard, 1984:184)

Only two of those aged 65 and over were described as being in full-time employment, and a further five in part-time employment. But as we have seen, the elderly population whose mental health problems had resulted in referral under the Act was primarily a female one, the majority of whom lived alone. The 1981 census showed that 76 per cent of men aged 60 and over and 61 per cent of men aged 75 years and over were married compared with 44 per cent and 20 per cent of women in the same age groups. Women live longer and are more likely to experience widowhood than are men. With increasing age, social visiting becomes increasingly infrequent and Abrams (1980) has highlighted what subsequent surveys have reiterated, that very elderly women are the most socially isolated group within the population.

Because women are more often likely to be bereaved we need to consider how gender affects mental health in old age. Loneliness and bereavement can in themselves be the source of depression, but the particular experience of elderly women goes beyond a frequently obvious and understandable response to loss. We have discussed how women's roles are seen to be embedded in their role within the family, but women more frequently than men experience an extended period of their lives during which their parental role is no longer required. Whilst such a role can be a source of stress for many women, it is this role which has been the source of their identity and purpose. Not only may they no longer have children and a spouse dependent on them for nurture, they may themselves be becoming dependent on children in a role reversal that can result in overdependency or conflict: 'For the minority living with children, the older women will have to face the conflicts caused by changed roles within the family – who does the 'mothering' and who is "mothered"? (Peace, 1986:71) It was indeed a minority of elderly people in this study who were in this situation – 6.9 per cent of women and 3.8 per cent of men, but it is nevertheless a potential source of stress that social workers need to be aware of when assessing elderly women who are dependent on their children.

Bereavement can come at the same time as the loss of a role that has formed the core of a woman's identity. This can lead to internalized feelings of being unwanted, in the way, and a fear of causing trouble for grown-up children with their own lives to lead. Women whose sphere and focus of activity has been home and family and who have lived essentially private lives throughout much of their adulthood may be less likely to forge significant new friendships amongst contemporaries once the nuclear family has dispersed:

> It does seem that the cultural definition of women as having meaningful lives only through a domestic setting in which they service others does have the effect in old age of removing from

frail elderly women who live alone the possibilities of investing life with real meaning.

(Finch and Groves, 1985:109)

In the previous section of this chapter we discussed generally the experience of those already living in residential accommodation when they were referred for assessment. The proportion of elderly people living in statutory, private, or voluntary residential homes was small: 10 per cent of elderly women were living in such homes compared with 11 per cent of elderly men. Very few of either sex were living with people other than relatives apart from those in some form of residential care.

Sheila Peace notes that admission to residential care has particular traumas and consequences for elderly women:

Although such a move is often frowned upon by both sexes, the transition for a younger, more active male, who may have experienced the routines of communal living at some stage in his life, may be relatively less traumatic than for an older, frailer woman who has lived a more private home-centred life. For many men such a move is also accompanied by the replacement of home care by women within the family, by predominantly female care staff within the 'Home'. For women the experience may be far more complex, involving not only the loss of home and community status, but also of their major domestic role.

(Peace, 1986:73)

Residential care has the potential for providing both companionship from contemporaries and freedom from the strain of trying to survive on an inadequate income at a time when the benefits of warmth and comfort are perhaps most important. Yet the benefits of communal living are devalued in comparison with private lives and one consequence is that both those providing and those receiving residential care frequently view it as second best. In reality, elderly people may share accommodation without companionship. The lack of positive models of group living makes it difficult for those providing residential care to provide experiences that challenge that view. A researcher who spent a week as a participant observer in an elderly persons' home wrote: 'Every day brought new revelations, such as finding that two elderly ladies who had sat beside each other in the lounge for two years, had never talked to each other, except to say good morning or good night' (Warner, 1987:12). The provision of material comforts may be at the expense of an ability to take and carry through decisions about even the most simple aspects of daily living.

Residential care also has the possibility of providing an environment in which medication can be controlled and protection can be provided. However, there was a suspicion in some of the descriptions of the circumstances in which elderly people were being referred that the possible outcome of compulsory detention was viewed almost as a punishment for difficult behaviour. Our concerns in relation to this are threefold: first, if behaviour cannot be contained within a residential unit, what additional constraints are assumed to be necessary and available in hospital? Second, are there features of residential accommodation that may exacerbate mental distress in their elderly residents, or at least render it difficult for staff in such units to acknowledge and address the distress felt by residents in their care? And third, might not the move to hospital add to the disorientation of an elderly person who has already been moved from their familiar environment and thus made the task of dealing with their confusion more, rather than less difficult?

The following example may serve to highlight some of these issues. It is taken from the description of circumstances provided by the social worker undertaking the assessment:

Gentleman who had been moved from one home to another – unable to settle. In his third Part III home, usually lasted six weeks before becoming unsettled. Had emerged a month or so previously that client was paranoid – hence his inability to settle. Subject to ideas that substances are being put in his food and drink. People out to kill him. Had attacked two members of staff who had been giving him a lift through town before weekend. No insight. Refuses to accept medication.

Whilst we do not have the full details of this particular situation to be able to judge the accuracy of the analysis given, as a description it does given cause for some disquiet. If the response to a resident who becomes unsettled in one home is to move him to another, it seems unsurprising that this could be interpreted as people being out to get him, and that it should result in aggression towards those who are perceived as moving him again. What it does emphasize is that staff working in elderly persons' homes can expect to be caring for people with difficult and sometimes frightening mental health problems. Unless these staff are given training to enable them to understand and respond to the particular needs of the mentally disordered elderly people in their care, there is a danger that problems may be made worse by inappropriate responses. The importance of this is emphasized by the fact that admission to a residential unit is sometimes seen as alternative to hospital admission for elderly people referred from their own homes.

As they are currently organized, too many homes for elderly persons are more likely to reduce than to contribute to feelings of self-esteem amongst their residents. Yet if such homes reduce people's control over their own lives and reinforce society's message that elderly people have no useful part to play and can fill no valued social role, depression or aggression are likely outcomes.

> In one example an elderly lady, who was very shy, felt she had been 'pushed into' the home by her daughter who wanted her house, and so felt very rejected and frightened by the prospect of moving to a home. Her response was to shut herself away whenever possible and be unpleasant to everyone so they wouldn't disturb her.
>
> (Warner, 1987:16)

Of the elderly people referred in this study, 58 per cent were already known to the social services department concerned. One-third were current cases. Thus many will already have received some form of intervention in relation to previously experienced problems. Research quoted previously (Fisher, *et al.*, 1984) suggests that such intervention will rarely have focused specifically on their mental health problems. Other evidence (Black *et al.*, 1983) suggests that they are more likely to have been allocated to unqualified or ancillary staff and that the focus of such intervention would have been on practical help.

Social work with elderly people has not achieved either the same status or priority as work with children and families, and it has not received the same attention from radical or progressive social work theorists (see Bowl,1986, for a discussion of this). A critical problem is the dominant ageist stereotypes that define old age as a period of inevitable deterioration and decline. Elderly people are seen as a problem simply in view of their numbers – the 'rising tide' that will swamp the welfare services, and on an individual level are seen to be unrewarding 'cases' since a developmental prognosis is considered to be unlikely.

Thus there is a danger that previous interventions may not have made a positive contribution to easing mental health problems amongst the elderly people concerned, and may in some instances have reinforced ageist stereotypes which undermine self-esteem. Ageist expectations of behaviour appropriate to old people may result in an inappropriate response from workers.

In the case of apparent dementia, an additional problem for workers insufficiently familiar with the specifically medical aspects of ageing, is the fact that the mental symptoms of intrinsic brain failure (dementia) can result from causes other than organic changes in the brain itself:

> The most common cause in daily clinical practice is probably the use of drugs prescribed for some other condition, which taken excessively, irregularly or inappropriately are harmful to brain function. Other common causes include heart failure, infections, renal and liver disease, diabetes, the abuse of alcohol, respiratory disease and various metabolic and endocrine conditions.
>
> (Gray and Isaacs, 1979:13)

What this implies is the need for a much higher priority being given to developing an understanding of both the social and physical aspects of ageing. In view of the numbers involved, this should be a vital feature in ASW training. A practical example of this is the training exercise based on findings from this project (Newton, 1988).

Outcomes for elderly people

There were 2,125 requests for assessments or for assistance with informal admission of people aged 65 or over. Some were obviously referred for assessment on more than one occasion during the course of the year. Less than half (44 per cent) of those requests resulted in compulsorily detention, although nearly two-thirds (63 per cent) resulted in hospital admission or in the elderly person remaining in hospital. In the course of the year, 944 elderly people were compulsorily detained under sections 2, 3, or 4 in 42 areas involved in the study. Elderly people thus represent 16.3 per cent of those compulsorily detained in this period.

In comparison with the population as a whole, it does appear that the use of compulsory detention was avoided more often in the case of elderly people. And following assessment for admission for each of the three major admission sections, the very elderly (those over 85) were least likely to be admitted, either compulsorily or informally. In part this was because guardianship was, as the Commission hoped, being used as an alternative to admission as well as being requested more often in its own right for elderly people. One example of this was the case of an 85-year-old widow who lived alone and had a diagnosis of dementia. She was referred 'Because her detention order was due to expire. She was confused and unrealistic about her ability to cope at home. She appeared completely without insight into her condition. She was also very confused and muddled.' The social worker undertaking the assessment described the options as follows: 'The alternatives were section 3, guardianship and that she be declared as an informal patient. In view of her confusion it was agreed that she should be made the subject of a guardianship order.'

In this instance, the major problem appeared to be that there was no-one to ensure that her confusion did not render her unable to look after herself at home. Guardianship *per se* may be unable to ensure the regularity of support required by someone in this position, but it does represent a commitment by the social services department that may have ensured that a high priority was given to her care. Certainly in circumstances like this it is hard to see that continued hospitalization would be likely to improve her situation and the option of providing support and protection for her at home may be more appropriate in terms of both civil rights and personal dignity.

Whilst compulsory detention was used less often with old people than it was with younger people, there were still a considerable number of occasions on which the social worker undertaking the assessment thought that hospital admission could have been avoided if appropriate alternatives had been available. There were 402 admissions where this was felt to be the case – 30 per cent of all admissions of this age group. And although a smaller number of the very elderly people involved were admitted, it was still felt that more of those aged 85 plus than of the younger elderly could have been kept out of hospital. So what were the alternatives that social workers were looking for in such cases?

In the first instance they were looking for more help from the families of the elderly people concerned. Family support was mentioned more often than any other type of assistance for both elderly men and women – slightly more often in the case of men than of women. After support from families, alternative residential accommodation was mentioned most often as a means of preventing hospital admission. One may surmise that these elderly people were perceived as needing a high level of protection and care for 24 hours a day, but not necessarily the medical treatment provided in hospital.

But a considerable proportion were perceived to be able enough to remain at home with support from social, medical, and/or psychiatric services. The GP was seen as an important source of support that could have prevented admission in approximately one-third of cases of both men and women. After the GP, support (in descending order) from social workers, community psychiatric nurses, and domiciliary workers, was seen as likely to have prevented the need for hospital admission. Attendance at day centres, out-patients, or day hospital services were seen less often as an appropriate way of keeping elderly people out of hospital, but were mentioned sufficiently often to suggest that a greater availability of such resources might have reduced the rate at which elderly people were admitted to hospital.

Looking at those instances in which hospital admission was avoided, results suggest that this may largely be because mainstream social-services resources are geared more often to the needs of elderly people than to younger people. The recipients of domiciliary services from social services are predominantly elderly people who are too frail or confused to undertake daily household and personal-care tasks, residential accommodation is overwhelmingly composed of elderly persons' homes, and day-care services provide occupation for those beyond the age at which paid employment or home and family care fill people's hours. Thus, when social workers were looking for some means to ensure supervision, protection, and care for elderly people suffering from mental distress, they were more often able immediately to identify facilities than they were for younger people. Thus in nearly one-quarter of cases in which elderly people were kept out of hospital, it involved the use of domiciliary support services. In contrast, such services were used in only 12 per cent of cases overall. Again, one-tenth of elderly people diverted from hospital admission were given some alternative residential solution to their immediate difficulties. Whilst still being a small percentage, it was nevertheless a more frequent option than it was for younger people assessed during the same period.

Our concern is that such mainstream resources may be insufficiently geared up to meet the particular needs of those who may be experiencing quite severe mental health problems in their old age. The appearance of domiciliary support as a substantial element in resources being used to prevent hospital admission highlights a fairly familiar situation in which workers who probably receive least training and professional support and who are lowest in the service-providing hierarchy, are providing help in some of the most difficult circumstances.

It is also clear that, even though other resources make a more frequent appearance in these instances, it is still the trio of family, social worker, and GP who are providing the means to prevent hospital admission in most cases. Thinking back to the case study presented in Bernard Isaacs' work (p. 153), assistance on a number of fronts might be implied in cases where the mental health problem is likely to be one of a constellation of difficulties being experienced. One could imagine a situation in which assistance with household tasks from domiciliary services, supervision of medication from a community psychiatric nurse, attendance at a day centre to relieve isolation and possibly to receive an appropriate form of therapy, with additional support and contact from family and from a social worker who might act as an advocate in relation to the other statutory services, would provide a package of care that could help overcome practical, psychiatric, and social problems. Such a package might provide the intensive multi-disciplinary help of the type discussed in Chapter 2, which has been demonstrated to achieve as good if not better outcomes than institutional care. But whilst 177 of those not admitted to hospital received social work support, only 98 received visits from a CPN and only 44 received some form of day care. The

mean number of types of support received was less than 3. This suggests that the concept of packages of care rarely achieves reality.

There was some variation in the type of alternative care provided to elderly men and women in the study. Family support was used more often with women than men, even though the women were more likely to be living on their own and less likely to have a partner. On the other hand, elderly men were more likely to be given some form of alternative residential accommodation and to receive day care services. Women were more likely to receive help from domiciliary services and visits from a community psychiatric nurse. Taken together, these results suggest that differences in perception dependent on gender are still present in determining appropriate ways of helping elderly people with mental health problems. Women were seen as best off if services and informal support were geared to maintaining them at home, whilst it was more often seen to be appropriate to provide an institutional response to the needs of elderly men.

We also looked at what happened to those who had a diagnosis of dementia and who were found some alternative form of care that would keep them out of hospital, since it was this group particularly who were identified by the Mental Health Act Commission as being unlikely candidates for compulsory detention. Alternative residential accommodation was proportionately more frequently provided to those with a diagnosis of dementia. They also attended day hospital and received other forms of day care proportionately more often, but the actual numbers involved here were even smaller. Nearly 30 per cent of those with dementia were given domiciliary help, but once again it was primarily family, social workers, and GPs who provided help in most cases.

So what do we conclude about the way in which the mental health legislation is being applied in the case of elderly people? Generally, we would wish to point to modest success in avoiding hospital admission (and particularly compulsory detention) as encouraged by the Commission. But we do fear that this is not necessarily indicative of well-developed resources that are able to help with the specific mental health problem being experienced. Rather, we suspect it is because there are simply more general resources for elderly people than for other age groups. Guardian-

ship is being used with elderly people, but not very often and not across the country. We also suspect that preventing hospital admission may often be accompanied by increasing pressure on the families of the elderly people concerned, often without specialist help that can aim to improve, rather than contain their elderly relative's mental distress.

RACE, CULTURE, AND MENTAL DISORDER

Ethnic monitoring was not commonplace in social services departments when data was collected for this project. Thus there was no agreed definition of categories to be used and little experience amongst workers of recording the ethnic group of people referred to them. Thus our decision was to use a simple, if crude, categorization: white, Afro-Caribbean, Asian, mixed, and other. We acknowledge that this disguises important distinctions. Particularly it means that we are unable to say anything about the experience of Irish people referred under the Mental Health Act and that this is an important limitation in view of other evidence of their over-representation in the psychiatric in-patient population (Cochrane, 1983).

Our study has confirmed that race is a key variable affecting experience of the mental health system. Within our study areas were parts of the country with very small black populations and consequently rare referrals of black people for assessment. In order to avoid distorting the comparative analysis of outcomes by including areas in which no comparison could be made, we selected the ten areas with the highest proportion of their populations of Afro-Caribbean or Asian origin in order to carry out a detailed analysis of comparative results for different ethnic groups. The discussion that follows is based on results obtained in seven London boroughs and three metropolitan districts, two in the Midlands and one in Yorkshire. All had black populations comprising more than 11 per cent of the total population according to the 1981 census, rising to over one-quarter in one authority and nearly 30 per cent in another (see Table 6.2). These proportions are generally agreed to be underestimates as they are based on numbers of people living in households where the head of household was born in the New Commonwealth or Pakistan. There is no direct count of people by ethnic group.

164

Table 6.2 Population of 10 selected authorities

Authorities	Nos of people in households where head was born in New Commonwealth or Pakistan	%	Total pop.
A	59,632	29.42	202,650
B	29,761	15.17	196,159
C	21,441	14.82	144,616
D	33,609	16.89	198,938
E	37,122	17.30	214,595
F	18,891	11.53	163,892
G	46,490	18.43	252,240
H	118,372	26.06	454,198
I	34,942	11.38	306,993
J	149,301	14.98	996,369
Total	549,561	17.05	3,130,650

Overall 12.6 per cent of referrals in these areas were of people of Afro-Caribbean origin and 6.5 per cent were of people of Asian origin (see Table 6.3). However there were important variations between these areas. The proportion of referrals of Afro-Caribbean people varied from 2.7 per cent in one area to 28.9 per cent in another, whilst the proportion of referrals of Asian people varied from 3 per cent to 13.4 per cent.

Table 6.3 Ethnic group of people referred (ten authorities)

	no.	%
White	1,404	70.1
Afro-Caribbean	253	12.6
Asian	131	6.5
Mixed	31	1.5
Other	45	2.2
Not known	138	6.9
Total	2,002	100.0

Within these areas the *rate* at which people from different ethnic groups were referred to social workers for assessment varied considerably. Overall the average referral rate per 100,000 population in these ten authorities was 116.7. But the rate of referral per 100,000 of the Asian population was only 54.3, whilst the equivalent figure for the Afro-Caribbean population rose to 204 per 100,000. A degree of caution has to be expressed about the

exactness of these figures in view of the impossibility of obtaining totally accurate population figures for the different ethnic groups. Some of the areas concerned were able to provide population estimates that give a more accurate indication than the census can provide, but not all authorities had made estimates of the ethnic composition of their population and in these cases we had to rely on census figures. However, the size of the differences is such that we are confident that we have evidence of considerable differences of the rate at which people from different ethnic groups were being assessed for compulsory detention under the Act.

Table 6.4 Source of referral by ethnic group (main categories only)

	White	Afro-Caribbean	Asian
Informal	11.5	14.1	10.8
Police/courts	8.5	10.0	7.6
General practitioner	15.7	9.7	21.7
Psychiatric Services	46.8	43.8	52.2
Social services department	10.5	13.2	3.2

Further differences are evident if we consider the origins of these referrals. Table 6.4 details the main sources of referral of people from different ethnic groups. In the great majority of cases the Asian people were referred to social workers from medical sources. Whilst the medical referral route was the predominant one for all groups, the majority was considerably greater in the case of Asian people. In contrast, Afro-Caribbean people were more likely than other groups to be referred by the police or courts, to be referred from within the social services department itself, or to be referred by family, friends, or by themselves. Reflecting these differences in referral routes, the Asian people were less likely to be already known to the social services department – 46 per cent were previously known compared with 38 per cent of white people referred and 35 per cent of Afro-Caribbeans.

In view of the different referral sources, it is not surprising that there was a smaller proportion of 'not specified' assessment requests in relation to Asian people compared with other groups, and a correspondingly higher proportion of requests for section 2 assessments. However, this was the only major difference in the nature of requests. Whilst the rate and the origin of requests